THE 7 WORST MISTAKES INVESTORS MAKE

THE DEADLY SINS OF INVESTING AND HOW TO SAVE YOUR FINANCIAL FUTURE

MAURY FERTIG

JAICO PUBLISHING HOUSE

Ahmedabad Bangalore Bhopal Bhubaneswar Chennai
Delhi Hyderabad Kolkata Lucknow Mumbai

Published by Jaico Publishing House
A-2 Jash Chambers, 7-A Sir Phirozshah Mehta Road
Fort, Mumbai - 400 001
jaicopub@jaicobooks.com
www.jaicobooks.com

Original English-language edition published by AMACOM,
a division of the American Management Association, International,
New York.

THE 7 WORST MISTAKES INVESTORS MAKE
ISBN 978-81-8495-270-4

First Jaico Impression: 2011
Reissued: 2013
Originally published as *The 7 Deadly Sins of Investing*

Printed by
Repro India Limited
Plot No. 50/2, T.T.C. MIDC Industrial Area
Mahape, Navi Mumbai - 400 710.

To my wonderful wife, Nancy, and children Zach, Nathan, and Shayna, whose support and love made this book possible.

CONTENTS

ACKNOWLEDGMENTS

This book began at the onset of winter in 2002 as I sat at my computer and attempted to articulate my investment philosophy. I believe that this book accomplishes much of that goal. My hope that is after reading this book you will have learned a few things about yourself and will have some tools to be a better investor. There are many people I wish to thank for their help along this journey from that morning at my computer through to the publication of this book four years later.

Thanks to my business partner and co-founder of Relative Value Partners, Bob Huffman, for having the confidence in me to start this partnership and his support for this project. To Bruce Wexler, who helped me develop these stories and concepts into the finished product, and to Steve Yastrow, who pointed me in the right direction when I had completed my first draft, but needed to go to the next step. To my editors at AMACOM, Jacquie Flynn and Andy Ambraziejus, who were strong believers in the book and were both great to work with.

I wish to thank my business associate Catherine Cannon and my son Zach Fertig, who created graphs for the book. To Bill McIntosh and Mark Field, who gave me a shot in the big leagues at Salomon Brothers in 1985. To my supportive clients that were there with Bob and me when we opened our doors with barely a working telephone. To my dad, William Fertig, who instilled in me many of the values expressed in this book. Finally, to my supportive wife Nancy, who put up with me working on the manuscript and never questioned the great deal of time required to make this book a reality.

Introduction

We are far more vulnerable to the seven deadly sins in the world of investing than we are in other areas of our lives. Most of us tend to abide by the laws of the land or the rules of our offices. We recognize that we can't allow our id free rein and act without thinking, or we'll get in trouble. For this reason, we generally are faithful to our spouses, try to be responsible parents, live within a budget, and subscribe to the values and norms of our places of business. We may take a rare break from living according to ethics and norms, consciously deciding to "go wild" for an evening out with the boys or the girls. The majority of us, though, go wild with certain limits in place. We may go to a bar and drink more than we normally do, but we don't get so drunk that we lose all control and start fights with other customers or drive home drunk.

One of the most accepted forms of going wild in a controlled way is a weekend in Las Vegas. For two days, we dream of striking it rich and spend our money on games of chance where the odds of winning are not good.

Still, it's fun, and it allows us to dream about great wealth and changing our lives with one roll of the dice. In most instances, these Vegas weekends are harmless, since most people place a limit on what they're willing to lose and don't gamble more than that amount.

When it comes to investing, however, we often don't impose a limit on our losses and treat the market like our personal casino. It is astonishing that many investors who are highly ethical and controlled in other areas of their lives lose all inhibitions when they become investors. They may go to church every Sunday and refrain from smoking, drinking, and other detrimental behaviors, but when they invest, they become greedy, overly proud, and envious individuals. Perhaps some people feel the need to escape from their well-ordered, tightly managed lives, and investing gives them this opportunity. Perhaps others have psychological issues with money, and when they are in their investing mode, they are working out deeply rooted issues. Whatever the reasons, investors are more vulnerable than most to the seven deadly sins. The normally modest man becomes overly proud of his investing and refuses to admit he made a mistake on a stock pick. The generally even-tempered investor vents his rage by sticking with a sinking stock through hell and high water, ignoring the logical part of his brain.

This book is for every investor who senses that there has to be a better way. It is for everyone who rues an investment made too quickly or gets excited too soon because of envy, vanity, avarice, gluttony, sloth, lust, or anger. It is for people who view investing as a way to achieve a long-term goal—paying for a child's college education, buying a dream home, retirement—and want to accumulate wealth rather than to make and lose money in a zero-sum game. Most of all, it is for those of you who recognize your investing self when the seven deadly sins are mentioned.

You recall the time your envy of a friend's investing bonanza caused you to adopt an ill-conceived strategy.

You remember how you protected your vanity as an investor by refusing to admit that you made a mistake with a stock and held on to it too long.

You regret how your greed caused you to take a so-called insider's get-rich-quick tip and put your money into an IPO that went nowhere.

You wish your gluttony had not caused you to invest heavily—and unwisely—in a dog of a stock.

You chastise yourself for your sloth—for your unwillingness to do the necessary research before choosing a fund in which you invested most of your retirement money.

You hate how your lust for a trendy biotech stock investment caused you to leap before you looked.

And you rue how your anger over a bad investment caused you to throw good money after bad.

If any or all of these sinful memories resonate with you, join the club. The good news is they don't have to control your investing, and throughout this book I'll offer advice that will help you manage your worst impulses. I'll also tell you stories that will illustrate the dangers of the seven sins and the opportunities that arise if you don't fall prey to them. In fact, here are two such stories, one that illustrates the dangers and another that illustrates the opportunities.

Mr. Wave and Ms. Calm

In October, 1999, two forty-year-olds, Mr. Wave and Ms. Calm, have $250,000 401k retirement portfolios. At the time, the world is caught up in market mania and the NASDAQ is still 65 percent away from its peak. Until this point, Mr. Wave had been content to build his nest egg through a mix of index equity funds and bond funds. Mr. Wave, though, starts reading newspaper and magazine articles as well as investment newsletters to which he subscribes, and he starts to believe what some pundits are saying: The tech stocks have no ceiling in the foreseeable future. More than that, he hears friends and colleagues boast about the killings they're making in the market, and he immediately becomes jealous. He starts doing calculations about rates of return, and he realizes that if he is half as lucky as some of his colleagues say they've been, he can retire in five years; he can buy the boat he's always dreamed of having; he can travel the world. Envious and greedy, Mr. Wave places 90 percent of his 401k in a mutual fund that invests exclusevely in growth stocks and leaves the other 10 percent in cash.

Ms. Calm, on the other hand, reallocates her assets as follows: 15 percent growth stock mutual fund, 25 percent S&P 500 index fund, 35 percent intermediate government bond fund, 15 percent real estate investment trust fund, and 10 percent cash. Though Ms. Calm is tempted by all the media hype about high-tech investments, she does her homework and heeds the voices of caution among more conservative investment gurus. Though she too has dreams that require considerable amounts of money, she reminds herself that she built her $250,000 nest egg relatively slowly and carefully; that she eschewed other "can't miss" opportunities that generally did miss. For this reason, she chooses to go with a diversified, relatively conservative portfolio.

By February 2000, Mr. Wave is congratulating himself on his choices from the fall. His portfolio is now at $350,000, and ten days later it reaches $380,000. Mr. Wave's net worth has increased $130,000 in just four months, which represents a return of 52 percent or over 150 percent on an annualized basis. For the briefest of moments, Mr. Wave considers cashing out, but he quickly dismisses this thought as cowardly and shortsighted. If he were to do so, he could not retire in the next three years, his new goal. He also might not be able to take the elaborate and very expensive vacation he has planned when he does retire. Though he recognizes the market cannot continue its upward trend forever, he convinces himself that the wave will continue for at least another six months, that he'll be able to spot the signs when it's cresting and that he'll have the good sense to jump off at that time.

Ms. Calm, on the other hand, has seen her portfolio rise to $260,000 during this time period. Though she naturally envies people like Mr. Wave, she is conscious of this envy and recognizes that though it is a very human reaction, it is not one that should influence her investing decisions. She contents herself, instead, with her portfolio having appreciated $10,000 in four months. In more rational times this 12 percent annualized return would be considered an impressive rate of return. When a friend chastises her for missing out on a once-in-a-lifetime market boom, she becomes angry and chides herself for being stubborn about her investing philosophy. Again, though, she settles down as she reviews her diversified portfolio and considers her long-term goals. The diversified strategy makes perfect sense as long as she keeps in mind what she wants to get out of her investing—a secure retirement, perhaps a second home in a warmer climate after retirement.

Now let us skip forward about five years into the future. On January 1, 2005, Mr. Wave's portfolio had slid to $196,000. Though Ms. Calm was also exposed during this period in which the market (as defined by the S&P 500) dropped 13 percent, her portfolio has appreciated to $347,000.

It is said that your sins come back to haunt you, and this is certainly true in Mr. Wave's case. Let us assume that after the dramatic drop in his portfolio, Mr. Wave saw the light, became aware of how some of the seven sins affected his behavior and became a more diversified investor. Let us further assume that Mr. Wave and Ms. Calm both have similar portfolios and manage to obtain a 7 percent return for the next twenty years, putting $10,000 into their accounts annually. When they reach retirement twenty years later, Ms. Calm will have $1, 752,000 in her account while Mr. Wave will have $1,168,000. If they both hope to live another twenty-five years and continue to earn 7 percent, Mr. Wave can take out $100,000 annually to live on while Ms. Calm can take out $150,000. While $100,000 is a great deal of money in 2006, inflation will erode the buying power down to $35,600 by the time Mr. Wave is 75. This assumes a modest 3.5% rate of inflation. If Mr. Wave wants to make up the shortfall between his account and Ms. Calm's—if he wants to have the same amount of money to spend—then during his remaining twenty years of work, he would have to deposit an additional $14,000 (a total of $24,000 per year) annually into his retirement account.

The moral of this story is simple: Even a brief period of sinful investing can have a serious, negative impact on your long-term financial goals. Being continuously conscious of the seven sins and vigilant for how they might impact your investing decisions is how Ms. Calm took advantage of the market.

Keep Your Wits About You When You Gamble

It's likely that more of us are like Mr. Wave than like Ms. Calm. Though we know cognitively that a diversified portfolio makes sense, we are vulnerable to the powerful emotions that come with investing. Our anger or vanity or sloth causes us to lose objectivity and perspective. Like Mr. Wave, we invest based on our dreams and egos rather than on our logic and long-term goals.

Imagine taking all the money out of your various bank accounts, stuffing the cash in your pockets, getting drunk, and entering a Las Vegas casino. As unlikely as this scenario might seem, it accurately describes people who invest with the "big score" in mind. Investing opportunities are intoxicating. Like a blackjack player staggering up to the table certain that his system will turn the odds in his favor, investors often believe that they have the system or knowledge necessary to beat the house.

Gambling is fun. Turning $10,000 into $50,000 in a matter of weeks, days, or hours is enticing; who doesn't want to strike it rich? But like playing the lottery or the horses, investing isn't a fair game. If you are fortunate enough to turn $10,000 into $50,000, the market will probably even things out by turning your $50,000 into $10,000—or less.

Investing for the long term can also be fun and satisfying, but in a different way. People like Ms. Calm who steadily increase their net worth in pursuit of an ambitious goal feel a sense of accomplishment when they don't panic in bear markets and don't lose their perspective in bull ones. They take pride in keeping their portfolio diversified, a challenging task given that a volatile economy can unbalance any portfolio. There is a tortoise-versus-hare satisfaction in eventually catching and passing other investors who brag about their big wins. And it is gratifying to stick with stocks, bonds, and funds that you have faith in, even when market forces buffet them. It takes the discipline of a true professional to stick with a stock that you believe in, but when you do, the rewards are both economic and intrinsic.

General Electric: 1995–2005

For instance, in the 1990s General Electric enjoyed a spectacular run where it began the decade at a split-adjusted price of under $5 per share and reached $60 per share in the fall of 2000. A combination of the tech bubble and GE's numerous, well-performing businesses helped it achieve this tremendous growth. Nonetheless, GE was hurt by the tech collapse and other factors and failed to meet lofty earning predictions. By February, 2003, GE bottomed out at $21.30 per share. At this time, the yield was 3.50 percent and the PE was just under 15 times 2003 earnings. The stock was trading at nearly a third of where it had been three years before, and media and Wall Street analysts had nothing good to say about the stock or the company. In fact, most investment gurus thought GE's future looked dark.

Less than two years later, GE had recovered 60 percent of what it had lost, earnings growth was showing signs of life, and the company raised its dividend twice during this period. Perhaps even more significant, everyone who bought GE outside of the height of the bubble period (late 1999 through late 2001) realized a positive return from the stock.

If your investing was ruled by one or more of the seven deadly sins, however, you would have sold GE before it made its comeback; you would have been angry at the stock for disappointing you; you would have been sufficiently vain that you couldn't tolerate having such a "loser" in your portfolio. You may also have been unwilling to buy GE in the first place because your pride wouldn't let you join the masses and buy a stock everyone was hailing during GE's ascent in the 1990s (it was too "common" a stock for someone who prided himself on finding the uncommon jewels).

My point here and throughout this book is that holding onto an investment you truly believe in—that objectively appears solid and able to come out ahead in the long haul—has its own rewards.

Some of you, though, may find the impulse to gamble irresistible at times. If you're able to manage this impulse most of the time, then here is a technique you might consider when you're unable to resist. Just like a responsible gambler at a casino, set a loss limit for yourself. Perhaps it's 5 percent of what you invest annually. As long as you keep the percentage low and resolutely refuse to exceed it, you can limit the damage done by your investing gambles and satisfy that itch you have to play a long shot or heed a tip. Remember, however, that when you engage in this practice you are making yourself vulnerable to the seven sins. Win a lot and your greed will push you to exceed your limit. Lose a lot and your vanity will push you to compensate for your losses and demonstrate you're better than you appear.

As you've been reading, you may have sensed the philosophical underpinnings of the seven sins approach. I'd like to make this philosophy as clear as possible so you know exactly how it translates into investing wins.

No Investor Is Without Sin, but All Investors Can Aspire to a Pure Approach

The seven deadly sins cause investors to violate two holy rules—at least two that are holy to me. The first rule is that you must always measure your "real" return—your return with inflation, taxes, and fees factored into the equation and without rationalizations—on investment. The second rule is that you must evaluate every investing decision in light of your long-term goals.

When you're in the grip of envy, sloth, or pride, you may think you're measuring real return but in reality you're measuring the return you wish you had or one that feeds your hunger for action. Subconsciously, you don't want to face the fact that inflation has rendered your return less attractive than you assumed. Therefore, you calculate your return in the best light possible. For instance, if inflation is running at 5 percent annually and your portfolio rises by 8 percent, you have a 3 percent real return for the year. However most of your gain was taxed as ordinary income and your net return is around 5 percent—for a real return of zero. You may also find yourself making excuses for certain losses and discounting them. For instance, your total portfolio rose 9 percent, excluding the 15 percent drop in one stock in which you were heavily invested. That stock dropped because the CEO was indicted for fraud, and you tell yourself that "it really doesn't count" because of this unusual, unpredictable event. You give yourself a pass on that loss and don't figure it into your total return. As a result, you conclude you had a very good year rather than a mediocre one. Your sloth may have contributed to your failing to do your research and realizing this CEO was a dubious character. As a result, you maintain an investing approach that is seriously flawed.

One of my clients, Skip, used to trade his own account aggressively, buying and selling quickly in order to realize short-term profits. He would often boast about his investing prowess and how he made $100,000 one year through his strategy. One day I asked him for a detailed accounting of his strategy and how it worked. He explained how he watched the market like a hawk and had developed an eye for when stocks were ready to rise or fall. As we talked, though, Skip told me that when he totaled his short-term profits at the end of the year, he didn't count the stocks that had lost money but to which he was still holding on. He maintained that they didn't really represent a loss because he hadn't sold them. At the same time, Skip didn't factor in the taxes he paid on his gains as part of the sum he had made in a given year. While Skip was a smart investor who did have a good eye for the market, his pride prevented him from being honest about how much money he was really making. When he finally confronted the fact that he was fooling himself and became aware of the sins to which he was vulnerable, he became a much more effective investor. He recognized that he had an innate need to "book a profit," a need fueled not only by pride but by greed and lust (he quickly fell madly in love—and just as quickly out of love—with certain stocks). Only when he faced reality—that he was often giving up around one-third appreciation by taking a short-term gain—did he change his ways.

All this brings us to the next rule: Long-term goals. Most people have investing goals that involve retirement, a child's education fund, a second home, or some other major life event. Making a conscious effort to be aware of these goals when considering investment options often serves as a governor on the quick-sell reflex. People who have long-term goals will think twice before selling; capital gains taxes are a good deterrent. There are exceptions to this rule, of course, since if a company or industry seems to be facing insurmountable problems and the odds of them solving them are low, then selling may be the best way to deal with a bad situation. Most people, however, sell impulsively, fearfully, angrily, and greedily. They are operating emotionally, and when they become angry at a stock or become lazy (sloth) about researching why it hasn't performed well (and why it may perform better in the future), they want to get rid of it. As we will discover, a long-term perspective will help you evaluate a poor-performing stock and increase the odds that you'll make the right decision regarding the stock.

How This Book Will Help You

Many investment books lure readers with "get-rich-quick" advice. This book is designed to help you get rich slow. In fact, it will discourage you from using various systems that sound great on the surface but entail significant risk. This is not to say that these systems are worthless. No doubt, some people who use these approaches do make millions. The thing to remember, though, is that in every casino, a few people get lucky and their numbers come up at the roulette wheel or beat the odds when playing craps. One person may pull the lever on the slots, lights flash, bells ring, and coins tumble out, but it may take another one thousand people before it happens again.

The core of the book are the seven chapters describing each of the sins. In each chapter, you'll find stories of people who were guilty of a sin and how it had an impact on their investing. You'll also discover stories of people who learned to manage their sinful impulses and how this helped make them better investors. In each chapter, I'll provide techniques and tools for sin management designed to make you aware of your vulnerabilities and minimize their impact.

I would also advise you be aware of all seven sins, even though some may cause you more problems than others. At one point or another, you will probably fall victim to all seven sins. Though you may have a particular problem with gluttony, for instance, the other sins may catch you off guard and corrupt your decision-making. By being on guard for all seven sins, you can dramatically increase the likelihood of achieving your long-term goals, and achieving them sooner than you may have thought possible. I have known many people who have been able to take early retirement, afford to send their kids to private rather than state colleges, take a year off to travel the world, purchase a luxury boat that they had always dreamed about owning, and so on. In other words, by following the seven sins strategy, they have been able to achieve significant life dreams and desires.

After the seven chapters on each sin, you'll find a chapter that focuses on applying the lessons learned to common investing situations. As I'll detail, certain events or environments make us even more vulnerable to our sins than we normally are. Receiving alleged "inside" information, experiencing disappointing returns, and other situations all make us more likely to make a mistake because of the sins. I'll suggest ways in which you can protect yourself in these situations.

The final chapter contains a sermon against sin and a list of ten commandments to help you avoid the highly emotional investing that creates big losses. It also takes a look at the future and how likely market trends and developments make a sin-free approach even more essential than it is today.

In this last chapter and throughout the book, I will demonstrate that this investment approach is trend-proof. It is as effective in a bear market as in a bull market. In a bull market, for instance, people are most likely to be greedy, believing that if they don't invest heavily now, they might be missing the chance of a lifetime. In truth, they often make mistakes of an investing lifetime. During a bull market, people often invest in companies with marginal financial records that they would shy away from in less prosperous times. In bull markets, though, the stocks of companies with underlying weaknesses can still skyrocket based on rumors and promises. In these instances, it is easy for investors to throw caution to the wind and jump on board. As you'll discover, the seven deadly sins approach forces you to subject your decisions to "screens" that filter out false optimism and other causes of buying frenzy.

At the same time, this approach will also serve you well in a bear market. While certain sins are less common during a downturn—you see less envy and gluttony when there are a lot of losers—other sins rise to the surface. Sloth, for example, often tempts the unwary during slumps. When stocks are weak, people tend to avoid checking their portfolio as frequently as in good times. On the worst days—when headlines scream about black Mondays and such—people don't even want to look at what their investments are doing. I know investors who devoted a few hours every month to checking on their investments and doing some research about them, then going six months or even longer without focusing on their portfolios. Out of sight, out of mind is not a good mantra for an investor. In fact, sloth is particularly problematic during bear markets. When price-earnings ratios are 10 rather than 20, this is the time to do your homework and find the nuggets. Fighting against sloth in bear markets might seem counterintuitive—when there is bad news, who wants to immerse himself in it?—but this is often where the investing opportunities are. This is where you have the chance to buy low and ride the wave upward, but you need to do some information-gathering and analysis before you are in a position to seize this opportunity.

Throughout this book, I'll point out opportunities that often are obscured by sinful mindsets. I'll also emphasize that opportunities are missed and problems are encountered because these sins are so powerfully tempting. One of the underlying themes here is that everyone, no matter how intelligent, is vulnerable to them, which is why it's important to be constantly aware of their impact on our investing behaviors. I have a good friend who is an esteemed professor at a major university, and as smart as he is, sloth had an impact on his investing performance. With a self-directed retirement plan, this professor had the ability to invest in any publicly traded stock with his funds. In the late 1990s, he purchased many rising technology stocks and within a year or so, he had $750,000 in his account. Each month he spent at least a few hours researching hot companies and executing trades. As the markets declined, however, his enthusiasm for trading declined. As the prices of his stocks plummeted, he decided that the worst thing he could do was panic, so he did nothing at all. He simply held on to what he had and refused to look at how they were doing or purchase any stocks. He figured that he would get back into it when the economy rebounded and his stocks were on the rise. For two years, he managed to avoid all the newsletters, magazine and newspaper articles, and other sources of information about the market. He also failed to track the performance of his funds. Two years later, the value of these funds had fallen almost $500,000. If he had simply made the effort to become aware of what was happening, he could have sold, diversified, and added investments that better fit the economic environment. The odds are that if not for his sloth, he would have dramatically reduced the amount of his loss.

Why I Am in a Good Position to Preach Against Sin

This book is based on my more than twenty years in the investment world. Having started at Salomon Brothers in their famed sales and training program (which Michael Lewis made famous in his book, *Liar's Poker*) and working my way up to Salomon's Managing Director/ Corporate Bond Sales in the Midwest and Southwest, I know the territory. I was one of Salomon's top fixed-income salespeople throughout the 1990s and led a business in twenty states that transacted over $150 billion of corporate bond volume, generated over $100 million in annual commissions, and grew at an annual rate of 12 percent. These experiences enabled me to build a certain amount of credibility as a professional.

When I left in 2003 to become co-founder of my own money management firm, Relative Value Partners, I did so with one objective in mind: To help people use the seven sins approach to build their portfolios in order to achieve long-term goals. Earlier, I noted how my professor friend was guilty of one of the sins. More astonishingly, many of the professional investors I worked with were also guilty of these sins, especially when they invested for themselves. I witnessed men and women who were highly skilled at managing huge investments for others become highly unskilled when trading their own portfolios.

I have had the good fortune of a highly successful personal investment performance. During the ten-year period between January 1, 1995, and December 31, 2004, my annualized average return was 16.1 percent. During that time, the S&P 500 returned 11.5 percent, the NASDAQ 11 percent, and the Lehman Aggregate Bond-Index 8 percent. If you had given me $225,000 to invest ten years ago, I would have given you a portfolio worth $1 million (though of course, the real return would be somewhat less after being adjusted for inflation).

Both in my own investing and for my clients, I have seen how effective the seven sins strategy is at building wealth over time. It is also a true hedge against those instances when the market behaves irrationally. Every so often, the market will shock investors; it will go down when all economic indicators suggest it should go up and vice versa, or it will enter the doldrums when all signs point to a dynamic market. The seven sins often strike during these irrational periods, causing investors to lose their ability to be rational analyzers (because the market is clearly behaving irrationally) and heed their negative impulses. The market usually behaves rationally, but when it does not, people respond in kind. They become greedy, angry, vain, lazy, envious, compulsive, and infatuated rather than coolly analytical, and above all, patient.

I hope to convince you that patience is a virtue when it comes to investing, one that can be a strong defense against the seven sins. Some of the worst trades and investments I've seen are ones made in haste. Admittedly, patience is difficult to maintain in the face of a hot market tip (or at least what is perceived as a hot tip). In the vast majority of cases, though, watching and waiting serve investors better than reflexive action.

To help you develop patience, let's look at each of the seven sins and determine which ones are most likely to cause you to lose your cool, your objectivity, and your perspective.

1

Assess Your Vulnerability to Sin

Wise is the sinner who knows his vulnerability to sin. Though that sentence may sound biblical, it is strictly "Fertigian." Awareness of how your impulses are likely to influence your investing judgment is half the battle. As simple as this sounds, though, most people have little awareness of their vulnerabilities.

Part of the problem is that we normally don't think about the seven sins in relation to investing. Instead, we focus only on the investments themselves. We become so caught up in charts and trends and gurus' advice that we fail to heed how greed or envy is shaping our analysis and decision-making. If you doubt this statement—if you believe that you're able to filter out your emotions from your investing—take a second and reflect on what money means to you. For instance, consider what money means to you beyond its ability to buy things. Specifically, when it comes to money, have you ever:

__ Been jealous because a friend was making a lot more than you were making?

__ Felt demeaned by a paltry raise or salary offer?

__ Derived great satisfaction the first time you broke the $100,000 income barrier?

__ Became incensed when your spouse spent money in a way you felt was irresponsible?

__ Acted irrationally because you felt you were cheated out of a small sum of money?

__ Behaved oddly (being a cheapskate or a spendthrift, for instance) when it comes to spending or saving money?

__ Felt your worth as a person was related to how much money you had (or the type of car you owned or the community you lived in)?

It's likely that you responded affirmatively to at least some of these questions. As any psychologist will tell you, money is as much a symbol as it is a financial tool. Logically, this symbol becomes extremely powerful in an investing environment.

The ensuing chapters focus on each individual sin and offer advice about how to manage it. For now, though, I would like to provide you with a general sense of all the sins and how they influence investors. I would also like to help identify the ones to which you're most vulnerable.

Descriptions and Monologues

Let us begin with a description of each sin and the internal monologue of the investor under its sway. As you read, think about if the description and monologue hit close to home (or if it doesn't feel like you). While most of us are guilty of each investing sin at one time or another, it's likely that two or three of them are more prevalent in our lives than the others. Recognizing this fact is a great start on becoming a better investor. Though it's important to have top-of-mind awareness of all seven—all can affect every investor—noting and defending your most vulnerable areas is a critical first step.

Envy

No matter how good an investor you are, someone is always better. No doubt, even Peter Lynch and Warren Buffett have momentary pangs of envy as the media lionizes the latest investment guru and touts his astonishing track record. It is perfectly natural to be envious, and it only becomes a problem when you're not aware of your envy or when you deny it. In the former instance, you honestly don't realize that a conversation with a colleague at work about her investing success is pushing you to make a particular type of investment. In the latter instance, you're buying a particular stock because your older brother did great with it and you can't stand to admit this fact because you've always had an extremely competitive relationship.

Envy is not a sin when you're conscious of your feelings and use them to spur your effort and creativity when it comes to investments. Envy may catalyze increased research or cause you to come up with an innovative variation on an investing formula. Envy damages your investing, however, when you respond to it without much thought and with reflexive action. When a hated neighbor flaunts his new-found wealth due to his successful day trading, you reflexively step up your day trading in an effort to get even. Invariably, the envy reflex is going to get you in hot water.

Here is the interior monologue of an envious investor:

> "I can't sit on the sidelines while my buddy buys a stock that triples in value. In the past, I suppose I've rubbed it in his face when I've done well in the markets, and now he's paying me back and I can't stand it. Even worse, he bought the stock after I told him I thought it was a loser; I insisted he was "taking a flyer" on something that had little chance of panning out. I've got to show him that it was a lucky fluke, and the best way I can do that is by picking a winner myself, something nobody gives much chance of going up. I've been thinking about some companies that have received a lot of bad press like United Airlines or AT&T. I figure they've been down so long, they have nowhere to go but up, and if they do, I'll look like a genius and my buddy will envy me."

Vanity/Pride

A thin line separates the confident investor from the vain one. Confidence is great if you have solid evidence for your certainty that you've made the right investing decision. False confidence, though, can lead to serious investing mistakes. Most of the time, these mistakes involve a lack of clear-headed analysis of events and data. An excessive amount of pride causes you to rationalize data that might make you look bad as an investor. It can also prevent you from taking good advice from experts.

I know an investor who believes that investing pundits know nothing more than the average Joe. He dismisses their recommendations, explaining that they have axes to grind and lack the objectivity to offer valuable suggestions. This individual feels that he knows as much if not more than the professionals; that even though he has a job in a different field (he's a corporate sales executive), his diligent study of and participation in the markets over the years makes him an expert. As a result, he refuses to listen to recommendations of professionals or even heed investment columns or newsletters, preferring to trust his own acumen. It should come as no surprise that he loses more than he wins or that he excuses his mediocre performance by claiming that he just missed a windfall here or a fortune there. He believes that sooner or later, he's going to strike it rich, and that he hasn't yet because of bad luck and other forces beyond his control.

Vain investors also are characterized by an inability to sell a loser. For instance, Jack buys stock at $30 per share in a highly speculative technology company with no earnings, convinced that he is one of the few who sees the company's potential. When the stock drops to $20, Jack is undeterred. He doesn't read any of the research available, including a report that suggests the stock was expensive even when it was at $10 and that it shot up only because of a new, promising patent. When the new patent doesn't fulfill its promise, the price drops to $5 as other speculators have taken their profits and moved on. Not Jack, though. He vowed to himself that he would not sell the stock unless it went over $30. This was a vow that had everything to do with pride and nothing to do with real analysis.

To get a better sense of what's going on in the mind of someone like Jack, here is a vain investor's internal monologue:

> "I bought Micron Technology at $40 per share, but they have missed their earnings estimate and the stock has slipped to $36. Other people might sell, but I trust my judgment. Just because the earnings growth won't materialize this year doesn't mean it won't hit next year. I know a good company when I see it, and Micron is a good company."

(One year later, the monologue resumes)

> "Now Micron is at $20, and I know earnings have been poor, but anyone with understanding of the industry knows this is due to a slowdown in the chip sector. This should not affect Micron for more than a quarter. I realize that most industry analysts have lowered their forecast for the next year and that my broker suggested I sell the stock at $30, but what does he know anyway—he was just looking for the commission. It's not that I'm reluctant to sell a loser, but I'm more reluctant to sell a company with the potential to be a big winner. I've found that the so-called experts tend to gang up on companies that perform below expectations, and I think the problem with Micron is that it raised expectations too high. I've been right about this type of thing before, and I'll be right again, so I'm hanging on to the stock, even if it goes below $10."

Lust

The sin here involves falling head over heels in love with a stock or a trading pattern. Even the savviest investors are surprised by sudden downturns or upswings. Love may be blind, but obsessive lust is even more blinding. I have seen investors continue an investing pattern that any objective observer would say is completely irrational and self-destructive. To someone in lust with a stock, however, this pattern makes perfect sense.

Lustful investors often are focused on stocks that have some added meaning for them. For instance, some people place a disproportionate amount of their investment dollars in company stock. They figure they

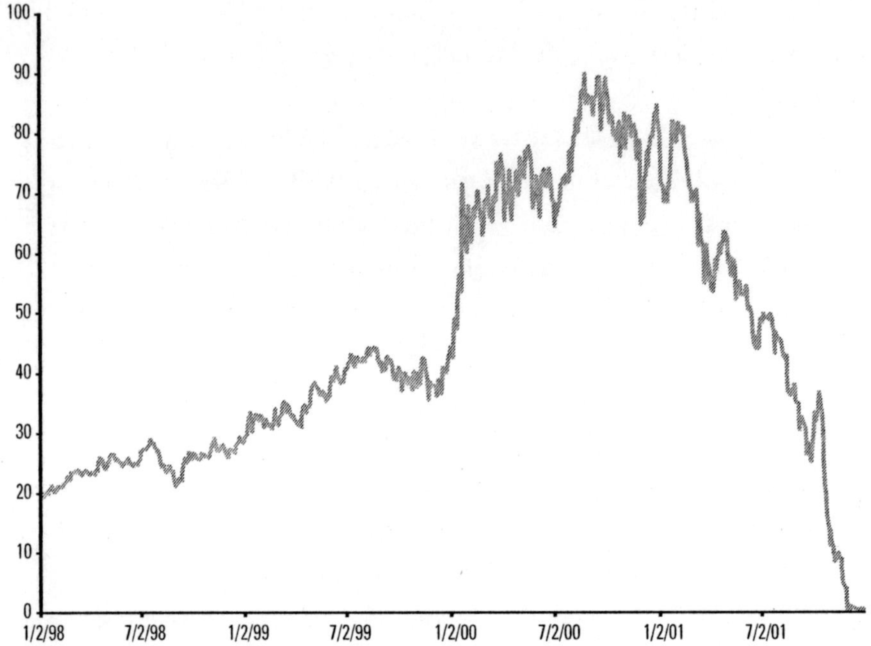

Enron: 1998–2002

work for the company, they know the quality of its products and services, they're convinced the leadership is stellar and perhaps they are able to obtain the stock at a discount. Too often, however, they see only the strengths of the company and none of its weaknesses. They forget that leadership changes, that quality fluctuates, the new competitors change everything. More than one story is out there about midlevel Enron employees who chose to put most or all of their retirement in Enron stock, saw the value of that stock increase quickly and kept it there throughout the company's debacle and were left with nothing.

Sometimes, too, people lust after certain stocks or funds because at one time, the feeling was mutual. A stock rewarded their choice with a dramatic upturn, and they believe it will continue on this path indefinitely—or it will overcome whatever downturns it experiences with more dramatic increases. Many times, these investors have a strong emotional identification with their stocks, and to consider selling them feels like a betrayal.

I want to emphasize that lust can also be directed at a pattern or system, not just a financial product. People hit upon a method of investing, it works, and they are convinced they have discovered a system for making money in the market. For instance, I've known more than one investor who has excitedly told me that his foolproof system involves only buying stocks when they reach the $25 mark and always selling them when they hit $30 (or some variation on these numbers). In fact, this system may work well for a while, and after they make money doing it with seven or eight investments, they are wild-eyed in love with the formula. Sooner or later, though, they will be the ones who feel betrayed. Eventually, they will buy something at $25 that never reaches $30 and goes in the opposite direction instead; or they sell at $30 and watch the stock rise to $50.

Lust makes investors slaves to their feelings rather than to their logic, as the following monologue captures (the year this monologue starts is 1998, which, as you'll discover, is a relevant fact):

> "As the father of a five-year-old, my primary goal for my investing is to save money to pay for my kid's college. At first, I did what everyone else was doing, putting money away in a separate account that was invested in low-risk vehicles. It was fine, but I wasn't getting much of a return, and at the rate tuition was rising, I figured I better find some other investment. Fortunately, I found Amazon.com. I put some money into this stock, and it went from $20 to over $100 in one year. When I look at an average 6 percent return of so-called safe investments versus what Amazon gives me, it isn't even a choice. So I'm going to keep putting money into this stock and I figure I'll have the college fund done before the time my son reaches high school."

(After the passage of one year, the monologue resumes)

> "This doesn't make any sense. I can't believe that the stock price has dipped to under $20. The way I look at it, Internet retailing can only grow and no company is better positioned to take advantage of this trend than Amazon. They are not like the other dot.coms that bit the dust. I know other people who have jumped off the bandwagon, but not me. I am

absolutely convinced that Amazon is going to enjoy the same huge growth spurt that it enjoyed last year. Yes, I'm betting my son's college education on this fact, but to me, it's the safest bet I can make. Amazon is the new IBM, it's going to be the bluest of the blue chips in the future. There's a certain amount of volatility that comes with the stock, but I've seen it go over $100 per share on two separate occasions, and I'm sure it will break this price again before my son is ready for college.”

Avarice

An old movie, *The Treasure of Sierra Madre,* describes how greed can warp people's actions to the point that they would rather die than give up their chance at making a fortune. In the movie, three prospectors seem like comrades in arms going out on a great adventure as they search for gold. By the end of the film, they are paranoid and murderous, unable to step back and see that their greed not only has turned them into evil men, but ultimately will prevent them from successfully capturing the gold.

Greedy investing may not have these dire consequences, but it can create lapses in judgment that seem dire from a financial standpoint. While ambition is a positive trait and allows people to set the bar high, greed keeps moving the bar higher and higher until it reaches an impossible height. A sure sign of greed is when you look at investing as the answer to your prayers, as a way out of a career that's going nowhere or as a way to purchase something that you normally couldn't afford. Our earlier Las Vegas analogy is especially apt with this sin; you view the market as one big roulette wheel and you can't wait to give it a spin and get rich.

Another sign of this sin is when you not only see the bet but raise it. For instance, let's assume you have put your money in a high-risk hedge fund (gravitating toward high-risk investments is still another sign). You have placed 10 percent of your net worth in this fund, and it has returned 20 percent for the last two years. You chide yourself for being too conservative; you think of all the things you might be able to purchase if you upped the percentage. In fact, you do the math and calculate the specific “toys” on your wish list you can buy if you place 50 percent of your net worth in the fund and it maintains its performance. You find the math intoxicating and make the 50 percent investment, ignoring the likelihood that your mathematical equation is fatally flawed, since high-risk funds rarely maintain a steady, high return for an extended period of time.

This monologue of an avaricious investor provides another perspective on what is going through this type of investor's mind:

> "I only invest in stocks that I believe will triple. People don't realize that you can make a lot of money fast in the market, but you have to think big. I like to buy stocks of companies where the share price has risen rapidly: If it has gone from $2 to $6 in a matter of days, what's to prevent it from going to $18? I catch the stock on the rise and take advantage of the momentum.
>
> Most of my friends invest in name companies like Johnson & Johnson and Exxon, but they're never going to make significant money from those stocks, at least in the near-term. Why should I wait around for those big company stocks to rise and split their shares? I admit I have the ambitious goal of tripling my money every year, but why shouldn't I have ambitious goals? There's no big secret to what I'm doing, except you have to be willing to dream big and take some risks. The reward of retiring before I'm fifty is worth the risk."

Anger/Wrath

Just as you shouldn't invest with lust in your heart, neither should you invest with hate in it. Unfortunately, the performance of the market, the opinions of the gurus, and the advice of brokers all may get your dander up. Please don't misunderstand about this sin: Great investors may be driven by a fire in their belly; they may be short with others and impatient with themselves since they are so driven to excel. Again, though, this anger can cross the line and be self-destructive. Angry investors always find something to be furious about, and it doesn't have to be an individual; it can be a particular investment, the economy, or even fate. Some people are so irrationally angry that they take a dip in the market personally and vow vengeance; they vow to beat the market after the market has beaten them. Others invest in what I refer to as a state of seethe; they are always looking for something to be mad about, whether it's their own misjudgments or a stock that fails to live up to an analyst's projections.

Jerry was the classic angry investor. He started buying Cisco (Ticker: CSCO*) in 2000, when it was hovering at a lofty $60 per share. At first he bought 500 shares, but when it dropped to $50, he bought another 500, viewing this price as a rare opportunity and the downward movement as a fluke. To Jerry, Cisco was a stock "you had to own at any price." In the money management business, Jerry was savvy about stocks and he was convinced that all signs pointed to Cisco as a stock that could only move in one direction in the future.

Up until this point, Jerry was like any knowledgeable investor. Cisco had received raves in the business press, and their future did look bright. But when the stock dropped to $30, most rational investors would have reduced their position or sold it all. Jerry, though, bought another 500 shares because he was furious at what he termed "an irrational market." During this time, every conversation with Jerry eventually came down to this topic. He would rage against the so-called investment gurus who had jumped off the Cisco bandwagon, claiming that were panicking. He could go on for thirty minutes about one pundit who said that Cisco was now falling to a fair price and its previous price was inflated.

When Cisco went down to $25, Jerry liquidated other holdings and bought 1,100 Cisco shares. Since then, Jerry has held on to his Cisco portfolio, despite the fact that it only briefly has gone above $25. His anger blinds him to the reality that Cisco's price probably was inflated earlier, and that he, like many other investors, were drawn in by all the favorable publicity. Because Jerry could not step back, distance himself from his anger, and admit his mistake, he lost a considerable amount of money that he'll probably never recoup, no matter how long he holds on to Cisco.

The following monologue will show you another way this sin manifests itself:

*Throughout the rest of the book ticker symbols are referred to in parentheses after the name of the particular stock or fund.

"I can't believe it. The minute I bought Intel, which everyone says is a great stock, it went down. I've had it for two weeks, and even though the NASDAQ trended upwards for those two weeks, Intel went down. So I've had it, I'm a patient guy, but I'm not stupid and hate to be taken advantage of. I'm selling it; I'm tired of these high-tech stocks anyway, they always disappoint me. I'm going to invest my money in stocks with great brand names, like John Deere and General Motors."

(After this investor makes this investment, the monologue continues)

"We just can't win against cheap foreign labor and the games businesses in other countries play. There's no way that I should lose 8 percent of my investment in less than two months. Deere and General Motors are solid companies, but the Asians and other third-worlders have created an unlevel playing field. Okay, if that's the way they want it, fine! I'll just find companies that have third-world country investments and put all my money in those stocks."

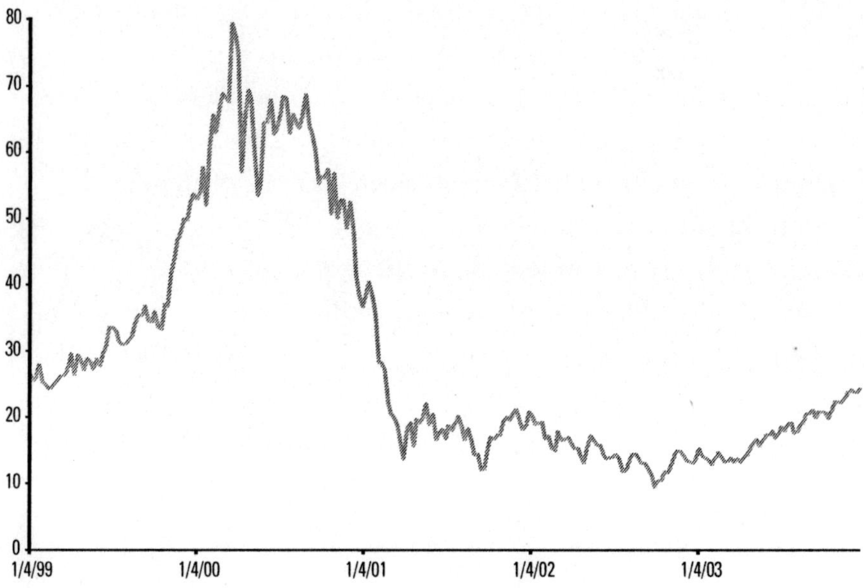

Cisco: 1999–2003

(After this investor does as he suggests, the monologue continues)

"I've had it; I'm going to write my Congressman! The minute I buy these third-world stocks, two of the companies are swept up in a federal investigation for alleged price fixing. Well, I'm not going to be played for a sucker anymore. I'm going to find one company that I know won't let me down, and I'm going to put all my investment dollars in their stock. I've done my homework, and I found a company with a great history, a service everyone needs, great advertising and branding. I'm going to put all my money in Delta Air Lines stock."

Gluttony

The previous monologue hints at this sin. Serial investing can be a drain both on your pocketbook and your mental energy. Good investors know when to leave well enough alone; they are aware that some of their best investments are ones where they just watched and waited. Active traders don't receive bonus points, and in fact may have to pay more in brokerage commissions. Short-term gains, too, can work against someone who trades too frequently, and the relatively new 15 percent tax rate on dividends is also something that should be taken into consideration. If that isn't a compelling yellow flag, consider that gains held less than one year can be taxed at a rate as high as 35 percent, while gains on stocks held for more than one year have a maximum federal tax rate of 15 percent.

More significantly, this sin causes people to sell their winners too early. Gluttons are always looking to the next trade and ready, willing, and able to sell early in order to realize a profit. Some people may not be guilty of any of the other sins—they do their research, they evaluate objectively, they make sound investment decisions based on the facts—and then they ruin everything by seizing any excuse to sell. Hyperactive investors tend to become bored easily and find no satisfaction in holding onto a stock. They want action, and for them, constant buying and selling is what they enjoy.

The gluttonous impulse is difficult to stifle, especially when you make an investment with certain expectations. For instance, in February, 2003,

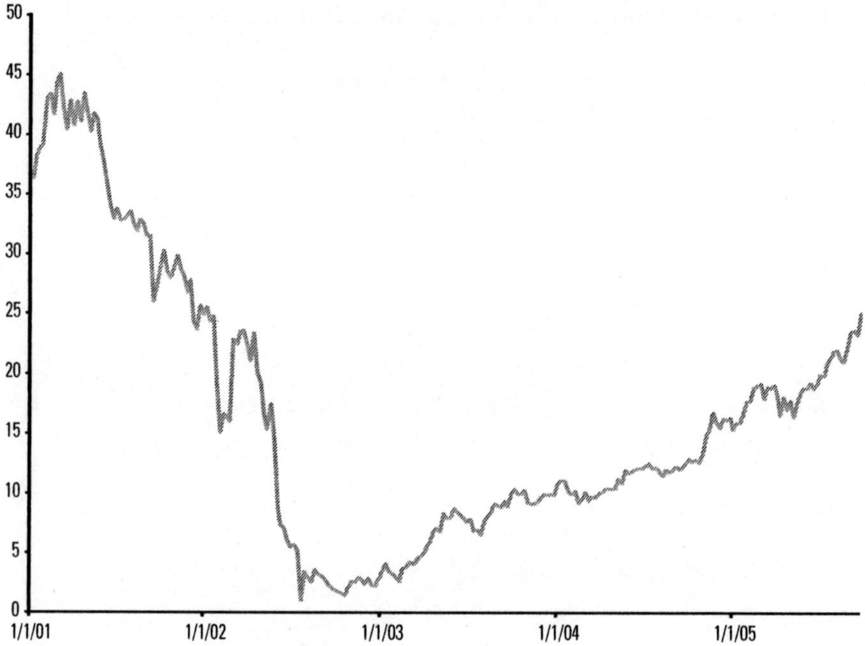

Williams Companies: 2001–9/30/2005

I bought Williams Companies (WMB), an overleveraged, troubled pipeline organization, for $3 a share. My expectation was that if the company could successfully sell assets and pay down some of their debt, the stock might be worth between $6 and $8 per share. When the stock rose to $6, I was ready to sell. Like a hungry man who had ordered his meal and had it brought to the table, I was ready to consume it and move on. Fortunately, I took some time and did my homework, and I saw that Williams' performance was excellent and the odds were good that the stock would go higher. So I stifled my selling impulse and waited. Sure enough, the stock went higher, first to $10, and then to $20. Each time, the glutton in me wanted to sell. Each time, though, I resisted because their recovery continued to be solid and energy prices were rising. As of this writing, I'm still resisting the impulse to sell.

Here is the monologue of a lawyer who is a day trader and is a glutton not only for buying and selling but for punishment:

"I just bought Apple and it is up $2, so I'm going to sell it and buy Oracle, which just dropped .50 so I can probably make some money trading it up a little. Sometimes when I'm engaged in trading, I get on a roll and I forget about everything else; I've been late to more than one client meeting because I get so wrapped up in trading. I think I'm pretty good at it, but over the past three years, I probably haven't done much better than broken even. Still, there are days when I anticipate the market and do really well, and I'm on a high. Even when I make mistakes, though, it's a blast. I have friends who make their investments in funds or blue chips and just let them ride, but I have no interest in that. Executing the trades is where the excitement is, making a split-second decision to sell or buy, using your instinct and seeing if your gamble pays off. In the past few months, I've probably bought and sold over 1,000 stocks. Sure, there are some I shouldn't have sold and I kick myself later, but that's just the nature of the game."

Sloth

Just about everyone receives tips about stocks. Sometimes the tips are from friends or colleagues who claim inside information. Other times, they come in more anonymous forms, such as newsletters or from investing gurus who have columns or programs. It is fine to use these tips as a starting point for an investing decision, but when they become the major factor in the decision, you're just being lazy. Today, just about everyone has online access to investigate the validity of a tip. Spending a little time determining a company's competitive environment and statistics about sales earnings or growth rates is advisable. Similarly, you can discover if management is selling stock, the consensus estimate for future earnings, and so on.

If you haven't bothered to look up some or all of this information, you're probably guilty of sloth.

Another form of sloth is failing to follow the markets and your investments. You may have done your due diligence prior to investing, but once you made the investment, you took your eye off the ball. Some people commit the sin of sloth after going into denial. Typically, this phenomenon occurs after a fierce sell-off. Rather than looking for opportunities, people can't tolerate seeing how much their portfolio's value has declined, so they close their eyes and hope that things improve without doing anything to help things improve.

In early 2003 at the onset of the Iraq war, the Dow spent a few months under 8,000. Market watchers offered doom-and-gloom forecasts, and people responded by avoiding the markets. Relatively few people did their homework and looked for bargains. No one thought to place the downturn in an historical perspective. If they had, they would have realized that markets often rebound strongly after a fierce sell-off. They would also have seen that quality companies like Alcoa and Goldman Sachs were selling for under ten times projected earnings.

People are especially vulnerable to sloth when the market is significantly down or significantly up. The overwhelming pessimism of the former causes people to stop investigating opportunities, since it seems like nothing is going up and nothing will be going up in the near future. Similarly, the unbridled optimism of true bull markets deludes investors into believing that everything they touch will turn to gold. As a result, they are less concerned with digging for information about investments since they are confident that whatever they do will have positive consequences.

Slothful investors wait for opportunities to come to them rather than seeking out these opportunities, as the following monologue suggests:

> "I am too busy with my job right now to spend a lot of time researching stocks and monitoring how my portfolio is doing; I figure that if I stick with companies that have well-known brands and a good history, I can't go wrong. I have put some of my money into a mutual fund, which I really don't have to pay much attention to because it's very well balanced and consists of mostly huge, conservative companies.
>
> The other day I bought some stock, but it was only because I was listening on the radio and some analyst was talking about how this is a great time to buy. He recommended a few different stocks, and I bought one of them. I figure if this major radio station employs him to give advice, he must know what he's talking about.

I just figure that investing is a crapshoot, and I can spend hundreds of hours trying to figure out what I should do or just use common sense: go with well-known corporate stocks and take the advice of the experts in the media. I figure I'm just as likely to strike pay dirt with this approach as if I devoted an enormous amount of time—which I don't have right now because of my job—to investing.”

Specific Sins Lead to Specific Mistakes

As you read through the descriptions of the sins and the accompanying monologues, it's likely that you had an inkling of the ones to which you are most vulnerable. You may have found one or more than one, seeing your own investing behaviors in the descriptions. While it's important to be aware of all seven sins—most of us fall victim to all of them during the course of an investing lifetime—pinpointing the sins that are most likely to hurt your investing performance is key. To help in doing this, I keep a journal of my trading activity. In the journal, I note where and when I first heard of a particular company, what research I did into it, the reasons behind my decision to buy it (or not buy it), why I sold it, and so on.

To help you pinpoint your vulnerabilities, I'm going to list some common investing mistakes and the specific sins that catalyze these mistakes. As you'll see, more than one sin can cause some mistakes, so you won't always find a one-on-one relationship between mistake and sin. Still, this exercise will help you hone in on your vulnerabilities, narrowing the list down from seven to one, two, or three.

INVESTING AFTER A RALLY HAS WOKEN YOU UP

Some people revisit their investments only when the market rallies 10 percent. They end up catching the market at a near-term high and only put their money in after the price has gone up. It is akin to buying a suit only after the sale ends.

Envy, sloth, and greed drive this mistake. When a rally occurs, you see others benefiting, envy their success, and want to get in on it.

You're guilty of sloth because you've ignored your investments only until the rally has roused you of your torpor. The slothful investor is one who doesn't pay attention to investing until *Newsweek's* cover declares a bull market.

Greed also prompts this mistake because you see the *Newsweek* cover and are convinced that you can find a way to make a fortune.

SELLING AFTER THE MARKET MAKES A SIGNIFICANT CORRECTION

Typically, anger is the cause of this mistake. When investors give up on a losing market and the downside volatility and sell, they usually do so out of anger. It is as if the market has let them down, and they're furious with it for doing so. Their anger clouds their thinking and one part of them believes that the market will never recover or it will take years for it to rebound. As a result, they often sell prematurely and lose out when the market rallies.

BELIEVING YOU ARE PRIVY TO A "SECRET" THAT WILL CAUSE A STOCK TO RISE

Greed is the culprit here. Typically, people receive a tip from the proverbial "friend of a friend" who knows that some little-known company is about to introduce a revolutionary new product, and they have a chance to get in on the ground floor. Some people receive tips from even more unlikely sources—cabbies, plumbers, bartenders—and take them as gospel. Generally, individuals who act on what they hear from these sources are greedy. They want so badly to make huge amounts of money that they convince themselves a dubious tip is valid; that an unsubstantiated rumor will cause a moribund stock to experience a dramatic price increase.

SELLING TOO SOON

Gluttony feeds this mistake. As I noted earlier, gluttons need the action that selling provides, and as a result, they sell too quickly and miss out on potential capital appreciation and dividends, and pay a lot in taxes and commissions. Premature selling often causes people to desert a winner too quickly.

DOUBLING DOWN ON A BAD INVESTMENT

This mistake also might be called, "Throwing good money after bad," and though a multitude of sins can catalyze it, pride and lust are usually the main culprits. Hubris prevents investors from admitting they made a mistake; they double and even triple up a bad stock to avoid facing their initial, flawed reasoning. People also increase their investment in losers when they are obsessed about a stock. For reasons deeper than I'm qualified to go into, some individuals become fixated on a given investment, absolutely certain that it's going to pay off in a big way, even when all the evidence suggests otherwise. Their lust overcomes reason, and they make the doubling mistake.

BUYING A STOCK OR A MUTUAL FUND YOU KNOW LITTLE OR NOTHING ABOUT

Who would make such a mistake? A slothful investor, that's who. Astonishingly, some people are just plain lazy when it comes to investing or they convince themselves that knowing a little is just as good as knowing a lot. When they avoid the facts—when they buy based on the skimpiest of trends or because of a system that is more voodoo than knowledge-based—they are likely to take a flyer.

DUPLICATING SOMEONE ELSE'S INVESTMENT

On the surface, perhaps, this mistake makes sense to envious investors. They know or hear about someone who struck it rich with a particular stock, type of fund, or investing strategy, and they decide to copy it. They assume that if it worked for one person, it will work for another. Of course, the fallacy inherent in this reasoning is rooted in timing: If it worked yesterday, it doesn't mean it will work today. Still, if you're sufficiently envious, you can easily overlook this truism, preferring the illogic spawned by an intense desire to have what someone else possesses.

Two Additional Variables

If you need an additional factor to help you determine your vulnerabilities, consider whether you're a short-term trader or a long-term investor. If you're a day trader, for instance, you probably love the action and the possibility of a quick profit, causing you to be vulnerable to gluttony and greed. If you are a long-term investor, lust and sloth are likely vulnerabilities. I've known a number of long-term investors who believe there is NEVER a good time to sell a stock. They are so obsessed with their buys—

usually blue chip stocks whose companies have stellar reputations—that they can't conceive of them ever doing poorly. Sloth, too, is a danger for long-termers, since they frequently are overconfident in their conservative strategy and don't monitor their investments carefully.

Envy, pride, and anger can beset any type of investor, no matter what his or her investing time frame might be.

Clearly, these guidelines should be taken with a grain of salt. I've known slothful short-term traders and greedy long-termers. Still, if you use them as an overlay with the other indicators, they may help you pinpoint your weaknesses.

The other tool that I will offer you has nothing to do with investing and everything to do with your personality. While you may display different traits as an investor than as a person, many times they are the same. Therefore, place a check mark next to the traits that describe you and then see how they correspond to the seven sins:

__ **A.** I consider myself a laid-back person who saves energy for things that really matter. For this reason, I sleep late when I can, do very little on weekends, prefer vacations where I can go to the beach and read a book rather than sight-see, and try to avoid any unnecessary tasks around the house.

__ **B.** When my neighbor gets a fancy new car or a friend receives a big promotion, I feel good for them, but I also find myself in a down mood and wonder, "Why not me; what did they do to deserve it?"

__ **C.** I tend to do things to excess, and I think part of the reason I've been successful in my career is that I can take on so much. In my personal life too, people like being around me because I make things happen and enjoy trying new things. I become bored easily so I keep my schedule full of activities.

__ **D.** People tell me I'm hot-tempered, and I have a reputation at work for having a short fuse. I've always been aggressive and a leader, and people respect that I tell it like it is; they also know if someone wrongs me, I don't forgive or forget.

__ **E.** I'm the sort of person who rarely tells people when something bad happens, whether it's an illness, the loss of a job, or the end of a relationship. I'm a strong person and like to project confidence and optimism. I find it very difficult to ask others for help, even if I need it, and I have trouble admitting mistakes.

__ **F.** I enjoy the good life; I try to buy the best whenever I can. When I was young, my goals always revolved around earning a certain salary by a certain age and acquiring certain things. I think this desire to acquire has driven me to succeed, but it also causes me to be unsatisfied with what I have and always want more.

__ **G.** It's fair to call me an obsessive personality. I become fixated on certain things and value them more highly than perhaps I should. If I go to a restaurant and like it, I'll rave about it to whoever will listen. I worship our city's professional sports teams and live and die with their wins and losses. I tend to use hyperbole to describe the things I like.

Answers:

A. Sloth

B. Envy

C. Gluttony

D. Anger

E. Pride

F. Greed

G. Lust

Now that you have some familiarity with each of the sins, your vulnerability to them, and how they may influence your investing, let's take a closer look at each sin, starting with envy.

2

Envy

The Stock is Not Always Greener in Someone Else's Portfolio

Everyone knows someone who has made an extraordinarily smart investment—the guy who purchased Apple stock during its first year as a public company or bought into a mutual fund just before it recorded the highest return in its history. If we don't know someone, we have read or heard about an individual who did extremely well—a day trader who made all the right picks or someone with a formal system that actually worked. In fact, most of us hear about success stories far more often than we hear about failures. The business media typically focuses on spectacular winning investor strategies rather than on spectacular losers. In addition, friends and associates tend to boast about their successful investments and remain silent about their unsuccessful ones.

As a result, we're envious. What do they have that we don't? Envy eats at us and stokes our competitive fires. We resolve to equal their success and go them one better. If a friend doubled his investment, we'll triple ours. If a business colleague bragged about investing in the hottest company on the market at its launch, we'll scour the new offerings and find the next big thing.

The problem, of course, is that our investing goal is to equal or exceed someone else's success. Instead of analyzing a given investment objectively, we see it as a way to prove ourselves worthy to someone else or our own inner critic. We copy strategies that worked for others. We take risks to prove we're as smart and savvy as someone else. We may not acknowledge that envy is driving our investing behavior—we may not even be aware of it—but it pushes us to make decisions that we would not otherwise make.

To give you a sense of how this is so, let's look at a cautionary tale about an envious investor.

Turning Green with Envy and Red with Losses

In the summer of 1999, one of my co-workers, whom I'll refer to as Fred, had the good luck to buy 500 shares of Ariba (ARBA), a computer services company for $70 per share. By early 2000, the stock caught an enormous bid and had not only split 2 for 1, but had risen to $200 per share. The $35,000 investment was now worth over $200,000 in six short months. In January, Fred wisely sold half the position for $100,000 and recognized a short-term gain of over $80,000. Eager to enjoy his investment success, he bought a new Jaguar convertible.

One of the equity salespeople, Kyle, could not believe his eyes when he saw the new shiny vehicle parked outside of Sears Tower (even though it was winter, the top was down). Kyle had been with the firm two years longer than Fred and his compensation from Salomon Smith Barney was greater than Fred's. When Kyle saw Fred, he began to grill him about the car and the investment strategy that had made this purchase possible. Fred lauded Ariba and how the company's software and network applications were critically linked to the newly exploding growth of the Internet. He preached that Ariba stock had only just begun to move and that he would never have sold the stock at $200 if it were not for his desire to purchase the Jaguar. At the end of 1999, Ariba was unprofitable, had sales of under $50 million for the year, but traded with a market (value) capitalization of over $10 billion. By comparison, Caterpillar, Inc., the world's leading manufacturer of construction and mining equipment, traded with a market capitalization of $16 billion, sales of $19 billion and had a profit of nearly $1 billion in 1999.

Kyle didn't consider the comparative merits of these two companies, nor did he undertake any other type of rigorous analysis. Instead, he was incredulous at Fred's good fortune and could not stand to see Fred make another $100,000 while Kyle sat in money markets earning 3 percent. Kyle felt entitled to a car equal to Fred's Jaguar. Even an investment professional like Kyle was unable to recognize his envy and segregate it from his decision-making process. In February 2000, Ariba climbed to $250 per share and Kyle's envy pushed him take the entire $50,000 he had in his money market account and buy 500 shares of Ariba.

By March, Kyle and Fred were exchanging high-fives as Ariba leapt higher and higher. On March 8, Ariba closed at $330 and another two for one split was announced. Both of them thought briefly about selling their stock, but each time they paused to talk about it, the stock moved higher. They went out for beers after work to celebrate their new found fortune. Kyle even stopped by a Porsche dealer to consider how he might spend some of his profits.

By spring, though, Ariba along with most of the NASDAQ began to take back much of the good fortune it had shared with investors. At first the sell-off was thought to be merely a pause in the market rally. As Ariba sunk every day, Kyle and Fred were in denial, refusing to sell the stock at the absurdly low price of $150! Kyle had many chances to walk away with at least half of his investment, but again envy was driving his decision process. If the stock recovered and Fred made more money after Kyle had caved in after sustaining a $25,000 loss, this would be the absolute worst scenario imaginable. This envy of Fred caused Kyle to forget that Fred was in a different investing position than he was; that even if Ariba went to zero, Fred would make $65,000 ($100,000 sales proceeds minus $35,000 initial investment).

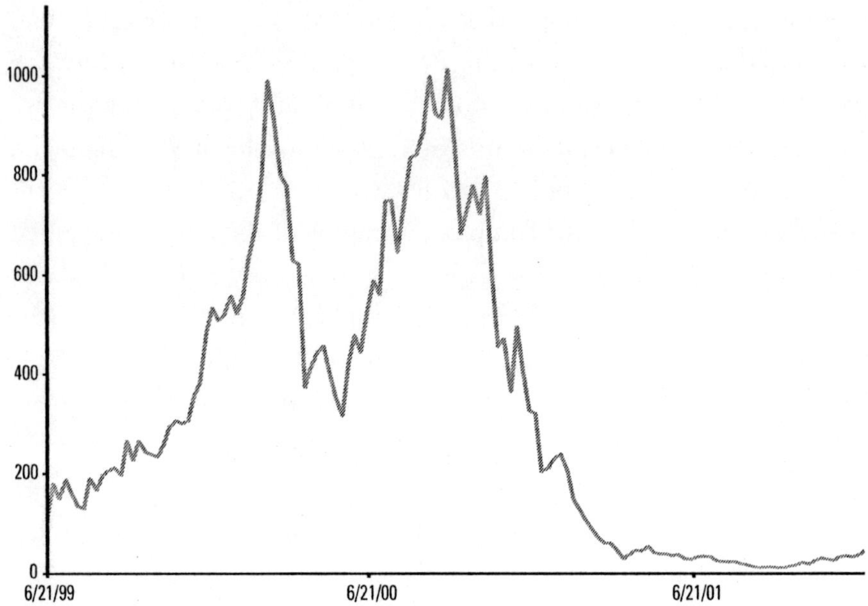

Ariba: 6/21/1999–12/31/2001

In April 2001, Fred and Kyle sold when Ariba was at $16 per share (adjusted for the April 2000 split). Fred's remaining investment was worth $16,000 and Kyle's was worth just $8,000, and Kyle suffered a $42,000 loss.

Is Envy Driving Your Investing Decisions?

It's natural to be envious of other people's success, but when envy starts influencing your judgment, you make investing mistakes. You may believe that you, unlike Kyle, can keep envy out of your decision-making. You may be convinced that your envy of someone you know or an investing professional is "benign," that you aren't hurt by your emotional response to another's success.

Rarely, however, have I heard someone in the grip of investing envy admit something to the effect of, "Yes, I put all my money into that fund that tanked because my tennis partner, with whom I'm extremely competitive, has been bragging about how the fund he invested in had the highest ROI of any fund this past year."

Envy is a sneaky emotion. It exists on the periphery of our consciousness, and it's often a feeling of which we're a bit ashamed. We don't like to admit that we envy someone who has done better than we have, especially if it's someone we don't like or to whom we feel superior. Consequently, we're as likely to deny we're in the grip of envy not only to others but to ourselves.

And that's when it becomes an investing sin.

To bring your envy to the surface, ask yourself the following questions before making an investment decision:

1. Is there an individual—either someone I know or an investment guru—who has made a lot of money with a similar investment to the one I'm contemplating?

2. Do I feel superior to this individual; do I think I know more about investing than he or she does?

3. Do I believe that this successful investor/guru is extraordinarily lucky rather than extraordinarily smart?

4. When I think about this person and his success, is my response primarily intellectual or primarily emotional; do I merely think that he's lucky or do I curse his luck and call him a "lucky so-and-so"?

5. Do I frequently talk negatively about this successful investor to other people?

6. If I had never met or heard anything about this individual, would I still be as excited as I am about this prospective investment?

7. If I make this prospective investment and it pays off in spades, would I derive great pleasure from informing this other person that I had picked a winner?

8. If I make the investment and it pays off handsomely but not quite at the level of the envied individual, would I feel that my

investment was "disappointing," and would I be tempted to try another strategy?

If you have four or more affirmative answers to these questions, you're vulnerable to envy as an investor. Admittedly, it's difficult to answer some of these hypothetical questions. Until it happens, you may not know if you would derive great pleasure from rubbing your success in another person's face, for instance. Still, you can use your instinct as a guide. If you find yourself smiling with satisfaction at the prospect of announcing your triumph to an envied individual, you can be fairly sure that envy is coloring your judgment.

Another way to judge your vulnerability to investing envy is to consider the following scenario.

Jerry is your neighbor, and he has been bragging to you incessantly about how he has made a small fortune in biotech stocks. You've seen Jerry's brokerage house statements, and you know that he isn't exaggerating—he has made a number of incredibly astute biotech picks. At the same time, you can't figure out how he did it. Not only did Jerry go to an inferior college to the one you went to, but he's an out-of-work salesman while you're a fast-rising executive. The other day, he gave you a tip about a biotech company that just went public, and you felt his manner was patronizing. He says it won't give you the spectacular gains of some of the other stocks he's invested in, but it should yield a decent profit.

Choose A or B related to this scenario:

1. A. I would follow Jerry's advice and be happy if the stock posts a decent gain.

   B. I would ignore Jerry's advice and attempt to find another biotech stock with greater upside potential.

2. A. I would invest a small amount of money in Jerry's stock to "test" his acumen.

   B. I would invest a large amount of money in an attempt to make a killing.

3. A. If the stock provides me with the "decent profit" Jerry predicted, I would call Jerry and thank him.

   B. If the stock provides a decent profit, I might call Jerry and thank him but would suspect he withheld telling me about even better biotech stocks.

4. A. If the stock goes down, I would be disappointed but wouldn't blame Jerry or myself.

   B. If the stock goes down, I would believe that Jerry has the magic touch and I lack it, and that if he were to have made the investment, the stock would have gone up.

5. A. When I see Jerry after he gave me the tip, we talk a bit about investing along with many other subjects.

   B. When I see Jerry, I obsessively ask him questions about his investing strategy and secrets, convinced he knows something I don't.

Obviously, the B answers are the envious ones. Later, we'll talk about how to deal with this envying impulse. First, though, we need to differentiate envy of an amateur like Jerry from envy of a professional.

You Can't Be Like Mike

If you watch CNBC or read any business publication, you are exposed every day to many stocks that experts own and may be touting. The *Barron's* Roundtable issue features several experts with their picks and pans and as many as 100 different stock recommendations in this issue. If you envy these very smart and wealthy professionals, consider the following truism: They did not make their millions by sharing their best ideas prior to having a full position in the stock. These pros are more than happy to share their picks once they have an established position. Sometimes the stocks have further to rise and sometimes they are running out of gas by the time they reach the publication. These pros seldom discuss their initial purchase price. They may still be recommending a stock at $20 that they purchased a few months ago at $10. It is not that they are trying to mislead you, but obviously your return might end up much different. For example, this stock rises to $25 per share; the pros will have realized a 150 percent return compared to your 25 percent.

Therefore, recognize it's highly unlikely that you'll equal their investing success by copying their strategies or following their recommendations. Of course, envy can cause you to overlook this fact and cling to the pipedream that now you know the professional's secret, you can equal or surpass him.

To disabuse yourself of the notions you might have about the pros, read the Berkshire Hathaway (BRK/A) annual report (www.berkshirehathaway.com) in which Warren Buffett shares his insights on the market and his companies. The report also discloses what stocks he owns and has been buying. You'll discover that as superb as his investment record is, it is impossible for investors to replicate by merely following his holdings.

There are times when the experts have bought the stock at much lower prices. They may still like the stock at the current price, but this is far different from actually *purchasing* the position. An expert might be touting a stock like Dell, which they bought right at $25 (much like Fred still liking Ariba at $200), and they like it at $35 when they are interviewed for a column. The stock has already run up 40 percent since their astute purchase, but you are just now being alerted to this fact. The pundit that recommended the stock can be wrong about further price appreciation, but still do just fine based on the initial purchase price. As an investor you need to make your own decisions as to a company's current valuation and if it makes sense to buy at the market price. The pundits may recommend lots of good companies, but be careful that the easy money in the stock has not already been made.

Envy, though, can cloud your judgment. Because of the power of the media and the persuasiveness of their writing, you may think to yourself, "I can do this! I can accumulate the same amount of wealth as Warren Buffett or any of the other superstars." You're jealous of their incredible success and the seeming ease with which they've made so much money. What do they have that you lack? Courage, you tell yourself; then you take the plunge.

In reality, here's what they have that you lack:

- Years of education, training, and experience as investors.
- The ability to spend the majority of their day researching, analyzing, and investing.
- A knack for reading the market.

It's fine to envy the pros, but don't think for a second that all that separates you from them is courage or opportunity. It's like thinking that all that separates you from Michael Jordan is desire. Therefore, put your envy in perspective and recognize that not only do the pros have talent but their success is not all it seems to be. If you knew all the hard work and failures they experienced before becoming superstars, you might not be so envious.

Just as importantly, stop your envy from leading to investing action by telling yourself, "They're not going to share their secrets to the world." Let's return to Warren Buffett to explain how this is so. When Warren Buffett begins to accumulate an equity position, he is not out in the marketplace telling the world about his purchase. He is quietly accumulating the stock and hoping it doesn't run up in his face before completing his purchase. Secrecy is the key to Buffett's ability to purchase a meaningful position at an attractive price. After establishing his position, he is happy to share it with the world. It also can be found in the various regulatory filings that his companies are required to file on a quarterly basis.

In his annual letter to shareholders, Mr. Buffett lists Berkshire Hathaway's largest equity positions. Now just because Mr. Buffett owns a stock does not mean that it is attractive. He will be the first to tell you that. He also lists his cost basis on many of these positions. Here is an excerpt from the 2004 chairman's letter:

12/31/04

Shares		(dollars in millions) Cost	Market Value
151,610,700	American Express Company	$1,470	$8,546
200,000,000	The Coca-Cola Company	1,299	8,328
96,000,000	The Gillette Company	600	4,299
14,350,600	H&R Block, Inc.	223	703
6,708,760	M&T Bank	103	723
24,000,000	Moody's Corp	499	084
1,727,765	The Washington Post	11	1,698
53,265,080	Wells Fargo & Company	463	3,508
Others		4,388	7828
Total Common Stocks		$9,056	$37,717

There are times when Mr. Buffett will add to an existing position if he deems it attractive, but positions such as American Express, Coca-Cola, and Gillette, were unchanged from 12/31/2002 to 12/31/2004. Mr. Buffett bought Coca-Cola at an average price of just $6.50 per share and as of this writing it trades at $45. Wells Fargo (WFC) was purchased at an average of $8.20 and trades at $60, for a 700 percent increase. The annual dividend of $2.08 based on his original Wells Fargo purchase price now amounts to a yield of a whopping 25 percent!

Now who wouldn't be envious of such great investment performance? I know that I certainly envy Mr. Buffett's expertise, but that should not drive my investment process. If I were merely to buy the companies, I would likely be doomed for mediocre performance. The timing of Mr. Buffett's investments does make all the difference in the world.

The logical question at this point would be if Mr. Buffett has such a great investment record, why would he still own these stocks if they aren't attractive for me to buy? The answer is that he faces two major hurdles when selling a stock that has performed well. First, there are capital gains taxes on long-term gains. Even at a 15 percent capital gains tax rate, this would be real money off the top. On his Wells Fargo holding, Mr. Buffett would have to pay over $450 million in Federal taxes if he were to sell the position. The second reason is that it would be very difficult to sell $3.5 billion in Wells Fargo stock at the current market price. If he were to sell even a small part of his holdings, it would have an adverse affect on the stock price. In addition, if the market were to become aware of his selling a major holding, that would further adversely affect the value. The only way to liquidate that much stock would be to sell at a price significantly lower than the current market.

Don't get me wrong—if Mr. Buffett were really uncomfortable with the long-term prospects of these companies, he would sell them below the market value and pay the taxes. He would evaluate tax issues, market liquidity (that is, the price at which he could sell), and long-term expectations for the company before deciding to sell. Only the last item would be relevant for

Wells Fargo: 1995–2004

Coca-Cola: 1995–2004

your consideration as a new investment. Just because a savvy investor owns a stock, therefore, doesn't mean that it makes sense for your portfolio.

In 1998, Coca-Cola (KO) traded around $70 per share and paid a dividend that was less than 1 percent. At the time, this was a stock that Mr. Buffett had already purchased and still liked the long-term prospects. In the 1997 Chairman's Letter, he spoke quite highly of Coke because of its "predictability of earnings." Back then, it was trading around $50. Buffett made his last purchase during 1994. The long-term prospects should not be confused with the short-term spike. In 1995, just three years before topping out in the $70s, Coke traded around $25 per share. On the back of strong growth in the late 1990s the stock clearly got ahead of itself. Simply because Warren Buffett had a position larger than $14 billion in the company, investors found comfort and plowed their money into Coke at $70 per share. Over the very, very long-term, the $70 purchase may prove to work out fine, but will it outperform the market and inflation? What was the opportunity cost of just buying the S&P 500 index?

Clearly it is easy for me to have 20/20 hindsight with respect to Coke. For Mr. Buffett it has been a great stock despite its sell-off. Even in 2004, after Coke has retreated 35 percent from its all-time high, the stock is up at a whopping 22 percent on an annual basis since his acquisition in the early 1990s, while the S & P 500 has grown at 12 percent over a similar period.

Millions of investors envy Mr. Buffett's billions and look at his investments as a way to achieve financial success. Now this isn't the worst starting point, but it is only a starting point! Coke may be a great company, but at what price? I frequently hear smart people refer to companies like Coke as great investments, but they are seldom cognizant of the key financial statistics. They are so envious of Mr. Buffett's foresight that they ignore due diligence and say, "I'm going to get in while the getting's good." Unfortunately, they are often too late.

Keeping Envy Three Steps Away

Whether you envy a professional investor or your neighbor, you need to segregate it from your investment decision-making. Here are three steps that I've found to be effective in keeping envy out of the investing mindset:

1. ***Examine your motivation deeply.*** What motivates you to make a given investment? Superficial answers might be, "I received a good tip from my broker" or "My research and instinct tell me it's going to pay off." What I'm suggesting is that you examine the reasons underlying these superficial responses. What specifically is driving you? Why does your research lead you to believe an investment will pay off? What about your broker's tip convinces you that it's a good stock? Be wary of answers that suggest you believe you will make millions, that a given stock will take off because the company has invented a product that is revolutionary. Perhaps you've hooked on to a one-in-a-million opportunity. More likely, however, is that you're in the grip of envy. When your motivation is to strike it rich, you probably have read about or heard from someone who has lived this lucky scenario. I'm not saying it can't happen, only that it represents envy's yellow flag. Envy causes you to transform a tip about a new product into news of a product that will change the world. You want so much for it to be that one-in-a-million product, you gladly invest your money in the company's stock.

When your deep motivation is to hit the jackpot, ask yourself if you recently read about or talked to someone who hit a similar jackpot. If so, envy may be compelling you to act as you do. Solicit advice from others you trust about the investment. Do they consider it wise? Would they make a similar investment? If they are wary of it, you should be too.

2. ***Demythologize the object of envy.*** We are vulnerable to investing envy in part because we make false assumptions and create fictional stories about other investors. We assume our colleague at work has a "green" thumb, which is why all his investments seem to pay off. We figure the investment guru whose newsletter we receive is so brilliant that he can chart trends in ways that most mortals can't. We elevate these people to a status that they usually don't deserve, and it's this elevated status that makes us so envious.

Demythologizing these individuals can make us less envious and less prone to investing mistakes. When we see that someone was merely lucky or his windfall was the result of years of study and hard work, envy often loses its power over us. Therefore, ask some questions and do some research. If you're envious of a well-known guru, you can go on the Internet and discover a great deal about his background. You may find that he struggled through some hard times as an investor, that he spent years creating and perfecting a system, that he was roundly criticized for inaccurate projections he made to the media. If you envy a friend or colleague, ask them—or people they know—about their investing history. Have they always been such astute investors or have they made their share of mistakes? What's the real story behind their "brilliant" investment or investment strategy; did they lose money based on inside tips for years until one accurate one came along; did it take them years of so-so investing results until they found a big winner?

3. ***Identify what you really want and if investing is the best way to get it.*** When you're envious of someone, you're actually envious of what they possess. Most of you wouldn't trade places with the person you envy for all the money in the world. You don't want to be your arrogant colleague who boasts of his gains or the guru who works one hundred hours a week and has pretty much forsaken a personal life. What you want is what they have. You want their luxury car, the security of having a pile of money, the vacation house in the country.

Therefore, when you suspect envy is driving your investing, do the following:

- Think about who it is you envy and what that individual has that you really want.
- Specify your object of envy—it may be something tangible like a house or a car or something intangible like fame or the ability to boast around the water cooler.
- Consider whether investing is the best way to achieve this goal.
- Determine whether there are alternative ways to get what you want: A savings plan, a new, better-paying job, a different career, relocating, and so on.

These four steps don't stop you from envying another person. Instead, they decrease the odds that the envy will get in the way of your investing. By taking these steps, you'll automatically look at an investment more analytically. Logic, objectivity, and research will be on your side. Rather than acting reflexively, you'll reflect before you act.

Envy, like all the other sins, is a powerful, emotional response to an individual who seems to have it made. Our egos and competitive drive place us in the worst possible investing frame of mind. We're especially vulnerable to envy if our own financial situation has taken a downturn. Recognize that you're most vulnerable when:

- You've recently lost money because of a bad investment.
- You've been fired from a job.
- You've just been divorced (and it's diminished—or will diminish—your financial resources).
- You need to come up with a sizable amount of money (to buy a new home, to pay off a debt, to send your child to college, and so on).

In these situations, you're most likely to envy others who have a lot of money or have made a lot recently. Allow yourself the luxury of envy, but don't let it cost you money. Box it up and keep it separate from your investing decision-making using the tools and tips found here.

Why Others Should Envy You

Envious investors view other people as savvier, smarter, luckier, and braver than they are. They feel as if they are missing something, and they look toward others to provide them with what they don't have. While it may be that Warren Buffett and other pros possess experience and expertise that rank amateurs lack, most investors have attributes that can serve them well in the markets. Some individuals are astute at picking financial advisors because they have insight into people and what makes them tick. Others know the business world well and have a good sense of the trends that have an impact on corporations. Still others are smart about economics and can anticipate how the Fed's actions will affect their investments.

Feelings of inferiority often reside beneath the surface of envy, so if you can recognize your own strengths, you can often manage your envy of others' strengths. Therefore, I'd like you to go over the following list and make checks next to the traits that describe your investing skills and knowledge:

__ A good sense of when is the right time to buy and sell

__ Perceptive about investments in certain sectors

__ Knowledgeable about the economics that govern market movement

__ A voracious consumer of information (books, articles, magazines, Web sites) about investments

__ Smart about picking the right investment advisors

__ Able to pick funds that usually perform at least as well as the standard measure for a particular investment category

__ Well-versed in market history; has a valuable historical perspective on market movement

__ Insightful about how an event in the larger world—a war, social upheaval, a natural disaster—will affect the markets

__ Has mastered at least one type of "more esoteric" investing (commodities, foreign markets, and so on)

__ Diligent about monitoring investments and has a good handle on how each investment is doing on at least a quarterly basis

Now look at the following list of accomplishments, and make a check next to the ones that apply to you:

__ Invested in a stock that was relatively unknown but that experienced a significant increase and became well-known

__ Got out of an investment in the nick of time, either before it started going down or after only a small loss

__ Own a fund that has experienced solid, steady increases over a period of five years or more

__ Has long-term relationships with a broker or advisor who has done an excellent job for you

__ Has maintained a diversified portfolio that is steadily moving you toward long-term objectives

__ Suggested a stock, bond, or fund pick to your broker/advisor that he had not thought of but that turned out to be an excellent investment

__ Refused to sell a downward-trending stock that your research told you would ultimately rebound (and you were right)

__ Bought in a down market when most people were selling and came up with a winner

Even if you only have one or two checks in each of the two sections, recognize that these checks represent strengths that other people would envy if they knew about them. Most people can be good long-term investors, especially if they use their strengths and hire good advisors and brokers to help them in areas where they are weak. The next time you're feeling envious of someone else and tempted to mimic their investing tactics, look at these two lists of investing skills and accomplishments. Ideally, this will blunt your envy of others and cause you to invest based on your own objective analysis of a given market and vehicle.

Finally, to convince yourself that you possess sufficient knowledge and skill that you don't have to envy others and invest based on their successes, try this experiment. Spend some time reading business magazines or looking at any media that contains news about companies large and small. As you read, you're bound to find stories about organizations that are doing exciting research, that are about to introduce new products, and that seem to have brilliant leadership. Search for organizations that are less well-known than the big Fortune 100 companies or that have recently gone public. Choose the ten you feel are most promising, write their names on a piece of paper, and pretend you bought 10,000 shares of their stock. Note the purchase price and the total value of each stock. At the end of each week for the next month, note your profit or loss in each stock.

My guess is that you will have chosen at least one huge winner. It's quite possible that you also chose three big losers, but the point of the exercise is not to come out ahead. In fact, most people will end up losing money if they did this exercise in real life. My objective is to get you to see how you can use your investing intelligence to pick a stock that might double your investment in a month's time. If you were to tell friends and colleagues about this success, they would be envious. If they suffered from the sin of envy, they might even try and duplicate your investment. Of course, you would not have told them about the three big losers.

I don't want you to be overconfident or think that you're so astute that you can invest like the best professionals. Instead, I hope you'll realize that you have specific strengths and knowledge as an investor, and that if you rely on that and combine it with a disciplined, long-term strategy, you won't need to envy anyone or try to duplicate their success.

3

Vanity/Pride

It Goeth Before a Fall

There is nothing wrong with being proud of your investing acumen. To a certain extent, all good investors possess confidence in their ability to read the market and make the right decisions at the right time. Everyone has an ego, and no doubt, the best investors display a bit more ego than most. If you have done well, you naturally take pride in your accomplishments.

Excessive pride, however, can destroy even the best investors. The Greeks had a word for this failing: Hubris. In Greek as well as in Shakespearean tragedies, the protagonist would usually ensure his demise because of this trait. From Oedipus to Othello, otherwise heroic figures would inadvertently set in motion the forces that would cause them to stumble. When their pride was controlled, it caused them to succeed. When it spiraled out of control and dominated their thinking and actions, it caused their downfall.

Investors suffer the same fate. This is an especially dangerous sin for smart, savvy people who have enjoyed some success in their investing lives. In fact, professional investors are as vulnerable to this sin as amateurs. If you are not aware that hubris is dominating your decision-making, you will move forward with confidence, unable to see that it is a false confidence. When you are so certain that your strategy is sound and your ego is so wrapped up in your investing success, you lose your ability to evaluate your decisions objectively.

To avoid this problem, you should meet an overly proud investor and see how this sin caused him to make a mistake that he never should have made.

The Man Who Had to Prove He Was Right

Marty should have known better. A seasoned high-yield trader at a foreign investment bank, Marty decided to make a big play in a little known or followed oil exploration company called XCL (XCLT). Plowing $250,000 into XCL, Marty boasted that he would get back ten times his investment. He was certain his knowledge of the oil industry would translate into a killing, and he bought maps of XCL's oil locations to the office, framed them, and placed them on his credenza, displaying them like a proud father.

Some of Marty's colleagues, though, did not share his enthusiasm for XCL. One of them, a specialist in the oil industry, examined XCL's financial statements and told Marty the company was highly leveraged, their earning prospects were bleak and that their company's future was riding on getting lucky with one of their wells. Marty, though, refused to listen. The more people insisted that this was a bad investment, the more Marty insisted it was a good one. Even as XCL failed to have a well hit and their price went down, Marty rationalized the decline. He would defend his investment, justifying the decline as "part of the price you pay for a stock with a huge upside." He kept insisting that these types of investment reward patience, and that he was not going to panic just because everyone else was. Ultimately, Marty lost virtually his entire investment.

As smart as Marty is, you would think it would be impossible for him not to realize that XCL was a loser. In fact, Marty is quite astute at analyzing

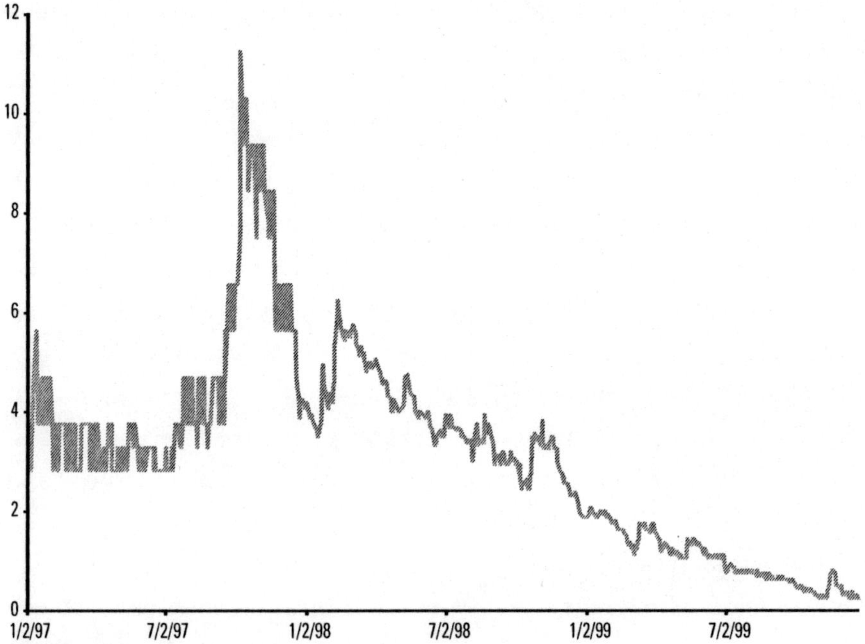

XCL: 1997–1999

investments. He is good at reading financial statements and forming accurate opinions based on what he reads. He knows what to look for when reading profiles of companies and interviews with their CEOs. All in all, Marty has high investing intelligence, but he shoots himself in the foot because of his pride. More specifically, his hubris prevents him from taking advice from others. It also encourages him to embrace his investing ideas without sufficient analysis.

For instance, in early 2001 Marty became extremely excited about AT&T. The stock had dipped from $50 to $23 over the course of the year, and he liked the prospects for the company as they had assembled a vast cable enterprise after its purchase in the late 1990s of TCI, Inc. Though the earnings had not yet materialized, Marty was convinced that they were perfectly positioned to take advantage of higher quality programming that was showing up on cable. He shared his belief in AT&T with his colleagues, insisting that this was a rare opportunity to get in at the start of a huge, sustained share price rise.

In fact, AT&T's integration of their cable businesses was not going smoothly, and its long distance phone business was shedding subscribers and revenue at an alarming rate. One of Marty's colleagues assembled research for him spotlighting these problems and why it was better to sell his stake in AT&T sooner rather than later. Marty, though, marshaled arguments against the logic of the research and his colleague's conclusions. He clung to the idea that its extensive cable holdings would far outweigh any problems in AT&T's other businesses; that integrating different cable operations was bound to be a struggle at first but a company with as much top-notch talent as AT&T possessed would soon figure out how to make it work. So Marty stubbornly held on to the stock, getting rid of it only after AT&T announced it was getting out of the cable business and selling its holdings to Comcast.

As you may have noticed, Marty was so stubborn that he refused to listen to advice. All of us, at some point in our investing lives, are obstinate and listen to our own inner voice rather than to the suggestions of others. A thin line exists between being confident in and committed to our investing strategy and embracing our own ideas blindly and inflexibly. To help you understand when you've crossed that line and committed a sin, here are some cautionary tales that illustrate the difference between a normal amount of pride and an excessive amount.

Why Overly Proud Investors Wouldn't Know a Good Tip if It Were Shouted in Their Ears

While Marty refused to listen to good advice, many vain investors not only don't listen but are suspicious of any investment they didn't dream up on their own. While it is wise to take everything you read and hear with a grain of salt, it is equally wise to evaluate this constant flow of information with objectivity, reflection, and research. The best investors know when they've encountered a piece of advice or nugget of information worth paying attention to. Overly proud investors, however, do the following with the investing advice they hear and read:

- Discount the vast majority of what they read in newsletters, magazines, and online

- Convince themselves that they know more than the authors of these articles

- Refuse to believe that anything that is public knowledge will be superior to what they can discover on their own

- Suspect that all brokers and other professionals are no smarter about investing than they are and that their advice is colored by bias or ignorance

It is astonishing how investors afflicted with hubris ignore advice that could make them significant amounts of money. In 2000 an article appeared in *Forbes* analyzing the merits of Real Estate Investment Trusts (REITs). Funded by the cash flow from specific properties, many of these trusts trade on NYSE or AMEX, but this investment can also be structured as an index fund that includes the entire market.

As the article pointed out, the Vanguard REIT Index had a yield of approximately 8 percent at a time when ten-year U.S. government bonds had a yield of 6 percent; it also discussed the safety of REIT investing in a volatile equity market.

Anyone who read the article carefully and did a little additional research on REITs would have realized that this was an opportune time to make this investment. They would have discovered that within the Vanguard REIT fund, stocks were trading at prices below the value of the properties, providing an excellent yield. From 2000 to 2005, this fund has risen over 150 percent (including dividends). During this time, most of the major stock indices declined.

The *Forbes* article passed on solid information that should have appealed to any investor's logic. Too much pride, however, short circuits the logic part of the brain. In fact, hubris twists logic and convinces us in this case that there must be a downside to REITs that the author isn't mentioning; that they want to sell magazines and perhaps also please real estate–related advertisers, so they are going to create a convincing arguments for this particular investment. The overly proud investor congratulates himself on seeing through this charade and being able to find his own investments without the "crutch" of a magazine article.

Overly proud investors are ingenious in coming up with justifications for their investment strategies. Their vanity drives them to create plausible-sounding arguments to avoid the conventional wisdom and go off on their own. For instance, Phil had been investing his 401k money for about ten years and had done well. He was convinced, however, that he could do better if he ignored the conventional wisdom about having a balanced 401k portfolio. In 2001, Phil reviewed a ten-year graph in a business magazine showing that small capitalization growth stocks had performed better than all other assets classes over the past decade. Phil decided that if he could emotionally accept the volatility of small caps—something he was certain he could do better than others—he would be better off in the long run. Phil was right that small caps experience a growth rate above the average of all small stocks and that it made sense to include a growth component in a portfolio designed for retirement.

Phil, like many overly proud investors, took these truths and formulated a plausible-sounding investment approach that allowed him to defy the conventional wisdom and demonstrate that he knew more than anyone else. Phil decided that rather than make a 20 percent allocation of growth stocks in his 401k, he would invest 100 percent in small caps. Phil reasoned that if it were ten years ago and he had made this decision then, his 401(k) would have experienced an increase over 15 percent per year.

A professional advisor pointed out to Phil the flaws in his reasoning; that the prospects for small caps weren't as rosy now as in 1991; that growth stocks no longer looked very attractive based on historical relationships to value and other asset classes; and that he would require a very good growth manager to handle the portfolio because the universe of these stocks is quite broad.

Phil ignored this advice, convinced not only that it represented the conventional wisdom of a balanced approach, but that it was overly conservative and better suited to the past than to the future. It should come as no surprise that in the next four years, Phil's portfolio went down in value, despite the fact that he was putting money into the account monthly.

Investing Behaviors That Are Signs of Hubris

Beyond refusing to heed good investing advice, the overly proud investor exhibits a number of other behaviors that get him in trouble. To help you determine if you are committing this sin, consider the following behaviors and if you regularly display some or all of them:

REFUSING TO SELL A BAD INVESTMENT BECAUSE YOU CAN'T ADMIT YOU MADE A MISTAKE

This behavior is different from holding on to a stock when all signs point to an upswing. It is also different from an investor who stays with an investment that is doing poorly in the short-term but has excellent long-term prospects. In fact, refusing to sell is often a virtue rather than a sin, demonstrating that an investor has patience and is taking a conservative, long-term approach. The sin of gluttony causes investors to sell at the slightest downturn, so I certainly am not suggesting that refusing to sell is always a result of excessive pride.

When it is a sign, however, it usually is accompanied by feelings of defensiveness about an investment. For instance, if anyone questions you about why you're not getting rid of a poorly performing stock, you would respond with an angry justification, insisting that you're certain that your initial logic was sound. You might also be so defensive about it that you refuse to discuss the subject. This defensiveness suggests that something besides logical analysis is behind your insistence on keeping a losing investment. Typically, you made the investment convinced that you had outsmarted the market, that you possessed knowledge no one else had or had conceived a strategy no one else had thought of. You congratulated yourself on your perspicacity, made your investment, and when it did not perform as you expected, your ego prevented you from admitting you made a mistake.

THROWING GOOD MONEY AFTER BAD

Not only does the investor refuse to sell a loser but he puts more money into it. This is an almost macho display of hubris (though one that women investors can also be guilty of), an attempt to prove to yourself as well as to the world that you still have faith in your judgment. Certainly it makes sense to bolster your position in an investment if you have solid evidence that it will do well in the future. Here, though, the most flimsy piece of evidence is seized and used to justify throwing good money after bad. For instance, the stock plummets for three weeks straight, and then it has a slight uptick for one or two days. The proud investor views what could be an anomaly as the rule and increases his stake. For the moment, this renewed faith in an investment feels good, providing the illusion that the investment is sound. Eventually, however, it will probably lose sufficient money that no amount of self-deception is possible.

POSSESSING AN UNBALANCED PORTFOLIO

While this can be a sign of other sins as well, the vain investor often feels that the rules that apply to other investors don't apply to him. As we saw in our earlier example, Phil did not believe he had to follow the conventional wisdom when it came to his 401(k). People who believe the rules don't apply to them are convinced that a diversified portfolio is unnecessary; that they know the magic formula to increase their return on investment beyond what others receive. They may have too large a concentration in a given stock or a sector of the market. They may unbalance the portfolio with too many utility stocks or convince themselves that companies like IBM and General Electric are impervious to downturns in the market and should therefore receive the lion's share of their investment dollars. They may eschew bonds altogether or err in the other direction and put all their money into the most conservative investments possible, having come to the conclusion before anyone else that the next great depression is just around the corner.

MAKING ESOTERIC OR JUST PLAIN ODD INVESTMENTS OR FOLLOWING AN ARCANE STRATEGY

The overly proud investor sometimes convinces himself that he has figured out a secret system or has discovered the "perfect" stock or fund that very few others have picked up on. While it is possible for an investor to hit upon a great new strategy or find a great investment before the rest of the world becomes aware of it, these instances are rare. Vain investors, however, relish blazing their own trails. They want to be the first to find the next Google and to say to others, "I was in on it from the beginning." This motivation to be a first adapter is dangerous, since it often leads investors into uncharted waters. It causes them to lose their objectivity when considering an investment, imbuing the unknown or seemingly unattractive stock, bond, or fund with greater value than it deserves simply because they discovered it. It also leads them to formulate strategies based on trends, mathematical formulas, or even astrology that may be original and creative but have little positive bearing on investment performance. It is almost as if these people take more pride in their innovative strategies than they do in their return on investment. While some individuals come up with ingenious strategies that actually work, the odds of a nonprofessional doing so are relatively slim.

I should emphasize here that esoteric or unusual choices are not signs of this sin when this behavior occurs infrequently or relatively small sums are invested. Some people take a flyer now and then, and if not much money is being risked, no harm done. When this behavior is central to an investor's philosophy, however, then it spells trouble.

If you find yourself frequently touting your discoveries to friends and urging them to invest in the next Microsoft or bragging about how the majority of your portfolio is invested in vehicles that no one else has ever heard of, you are probably guilty of hubris.

INVEST WITH CONFIDENCE LEAVENED WITH HUMILITY

Sooner or later, the market humbles everyone. This doesn't mean you should approach investing with fear and uncertainty, but a wise investor recognizes that even the pros make mistakes and that a willingness to cut losses quickly and absorb and analyze information will serve him well. Walking the fine line between humility and confidence—and between pride and self-questioning—can be difficult for everyone, but especially for investors guilty of this sin. To make it a bit easier, try following these steps:

1. ***Make a concerted effort to seek advice and knowledge, and try to take pride in your ability to discern useful from useless information.*** As a professional investment advisor, I experience moments when I wonder if it's worth it to seek additional information and opinions. After all, I've been investing for many years, I've been very successful, why not just trust my experience and instincts to guide my recommendations. In these moments, I remind myself of a few simple facts: Thousands of U.S. stocks are traded on various exchanges; adding in foreign markets and just considering equity and fixed income vehicles, an infinite number of ways to build a portfolio exist.

No professional can stay abreast of all this information without reading appropriate publications and listening to advice (through seminars, discussions with other professionals, and so on). Because something new is always emerging and changes are always happening, you may need to see an article about the relative value of large capitalization stocks for it to catch your attention or have a colleague inform you about the attractiveness of the Korean equity market after a 15 percent sell-off before you capitalize on it.

Recognize, therefore, that a wealth of information exists that is greater than your own personal knowledge. Make it a regular habit to read an article or newsletter, visit a Web site, and talk to someone whose investing expertise you respect at least once a week. Use your own analytical ability to decide what you hear and read is worth acting upon. The best investors are not lone rangers but people who are connected to information networks and skilled at interpreting the data that comes across their desks.

2. ***Substitute change-awareness for ego in making investment decisions.*** Many overly proud people are good investors, and they often display financial intelligence in their initial decisions. Problems crop up,

however, when situations change and they cannot back off their original stance because it threatens their ego. They go from good to bad investors because they fail to recognize that change has flawed their investment.

Change can be your friend or enemy, but you can only make it the former if you accept that it can make a right move a wrong one. As relationships between stocks and sectors move, so do the prospective returns of a sector. For example, if you buy a large bank stock at a price-to-earnings ratio of 12, this is usually a more attractive investment in an environment when ten-year U.S. government bond yields are at 4 percent rather than at 6 percent.

Recognize that you are not stupid because a good investment turns bad. Change-related factors are beyond your control, and smart investors make sure they are aware of changes and limit their losses, even if it means selling at a loss. They refuse to "save face" by clinging to a bad investment and hoping against hope that it turns around.

In 2002 I purchased Qwest Communication. Qwest, a former regional Bell holding company that provided wired telephone service to the Western U.S., seemed to have potential for deriving additional revenue beyond its traditional telephone services. The stock had been caught up in the tech bubble and traded over $60 per share in 2000. At $10 per share, Qwest was much less expensive than the larger phone companies on a per-access line basis. I was pleased with the prospects for the stock over the next twelve to eighteen months.

A few months later, though, I came across research highlighting the fact that Qwest was struggling to deal with an enormous debt load and was losing traditional customers rapidly. I sold the stock at $8, a 20 percent loss. I did not enjoy losing a significant amount of money in only a few months and admitting to myself that I probably should have learned more before making the investment, but changing circumstances made it imperative to get rid of the stock. Shortly thereafter, the stock dropped below $5 and stayed in that range for the next few years.

3. ***Don't try to outsmart the market.*** This type of thinking is akin to our earlier Las Vegas analogy: If you believe you can beat the house at their game, you are in for a rude awakening. You may be the best investor on the face of the earth, but your pride can turn you into one of the worst. No matter how much knowledge you possess or how good your instincts are, your hubris will sabotage your best efforts.

Therefore, approach the market with humility. This does not mean you should start doubting your abilities but that you should recognize you are dealing with a force that at times is inscrutable and unpredictable. Adopting a Zen-like attitude—recognizing that you are a speck in the universe of the market—puts things in perspective. The best investors really do go with the flow; they are open-minded, flexible, and contemplative. They are in tune with the market, understanding it as well as they are able and are attuned to its nuances. They are not so presumptuous as to believe that they can stay one step ahead of the market. Instead, they attempt to move in harmony with it.

If all this sounds a bit too spiritual for you, look at this step as a method to manage your pride so it doesn't get you into trouble. Think about the ways you may have attempted to outsmart the market in the past—creating a new investment strategy and following it rigidly, making unusual, esoteric investments, being certain you can predict what the market will do—and resolve to manage these impulses. Focus on using your skills and intelligence to take advantage of what the market gives you and be willing to change direction if the market indicates this is the wise course of action.

Two Scenarios

To help you put these two steps to work, I'm going to present you with two scenarios. After reading each, determine how you might have acted differently with the previous lessons in mind. Then look at how a good investor manages his pride and avoids the mistakes these vain investors made.

Scenario #1

Tom, a successful investor, was actively trading stocks throughout the 1990s, but toward the end of the decade he was burned once too often and decided he would pursue a strategy in which he avoided the equity market.

He put all his money in a short-term municipal bond fund, receiving a 3 percent, tax-free return. Shortly after making this move, the equity market experienced a severe correction and decreased 40 percent (as measured by the S&P 500). Tom congratulated himself on his foresight and didn't hesitate to tell his friends—some of whom had advised against avoiding the equity market—that he had read the market and made the right decision.

Over time, of course, the market rebounded and Tom saw people he knew whose portfolios grew at a much faster clip than his did. When friends would tell him he should have some equities as an inflation hedge or gave him studies that supported dollar-cost averaging, Tom dismissed their suggestions. During bull markets, Tom would sometimes wonder if he should get back into equities, but every time they experienced a sell off, he would feel like a genius. In his mind, Tom had concluded that equities were not what they were cracked up to be and never would be what they once were. Though his conclusions were based on a hodgepodge of information and his own theorizing, he was convinced that he was savvier than others and enjoyed pointing out his savvy whenever stocks were doing poorly.

WHAT YOU SHOULD DO IF YOU'RE IN TOM'S PLACE

When you start considering pulling out of the equity market, the first thing you should do is some research to consider whether your brilliant analysis of the markets and your strategy in response to this analysis makes sense. In this instance, you would discover an overwhelming amount of opinion favoring balanced portfolios in any type of market, especially for long-term investors. Many times, the weight of overwhelming evidence can counteract the pride people take in their investing schemes. Sometimes, one compelling piece of data can penetrate the mind fog that pride creates. For instance, if you were researching this subject, you might come across an Ibbotson study indicating that seventy-nine months account for the entire return on equities over the past seventy-five years. In other words, if you step out of the market during the 9 percent of the time the market rallies, you would have missed the market's upside performance. You would have also uncovered irrefutable evidence that over the long term, stocks always trend upwards. You would grasp that as long as you stay in the game long term, you're bound to win. Keep in mind that there have been periods as long as 15 years when market returns were negligible. Excessive pride may distort your judgment, but some startling facts may bring you back to reality.

Scenario #2

Hal is an entrepreneur who has built his business from scratch and takes a great deal of pride in his financial acumen. Over the years, he has handled all his investments himself and tells friends that all it takes is a little work and creativity and anyone can be a successful investor. Though Hal has not exactly been successful—his investing often ends up being a zero-sum game—he takes great pride in his ability to find unusual investments. At more than one cocktail party, he has put the guests to sleep, lecturing about one highly technical investing approach or another.

In the spring of 2002, Hal decided Sirius Satellite Radio stock was overvalued after reviewing their revenue stream and cost of acquiring subscribers. Based on this review, Hal implemented a plan to short a position of 10,000 shares at $5 per share. Over the next few years, the stock dropped to $2 a share and Hal was enormously pleased with his foresight. Convinced that the stock was still too expensive at its current price, Hal shorted another 50,000 shares at $2. He was positive that the company wouldn't make it, and that when it went under, he would clear a total of $150,000 in profit.

Hal's pride in his initial success prevented him from taking a step back and reassessing his initial analysis. Though Hal did a small amount of research before making his second investment, he quickly rationalized every positive piece about Sirius's future. Hal had read speculative reports that one of the Big Three automakers was considering a deal to put Sirius in all their vehicles, but he was sure these reports were false, since he could not imagine people paying for a service that they received for free. In fact, the entire basis for his investment was his certainty that the vast majority of people would reflexively resist the concept of paying

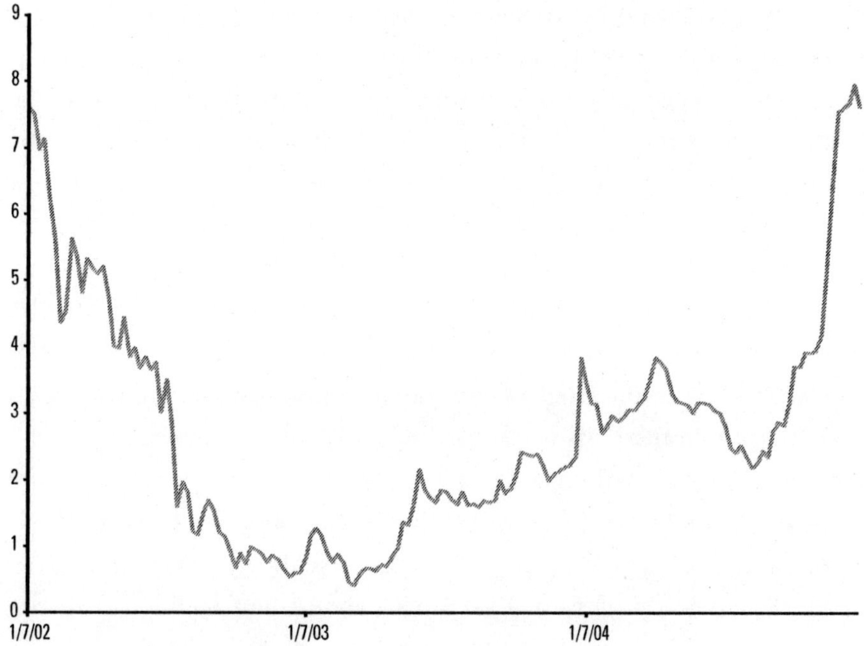

Sirius Satellite Radio: 2002–2004

for additional radio services. As Hal jokingly told his friends, "That company has made a serious miscalculation."

The joke, though, was on Hal when after the stock bottomed out at $1 in May, 2003, it started a climb that reached over $9 in December 2004. When a short goes against you, two problems exist: 1) You must post margin (cash or securities) for the difference the stock has appreciated to make up that difference—Hal had to come up with over $400,000 or the broker would buy the stock back and Hal would face a loss. 2) You must continue to "borrow" the stock. When a stock is heavily shorted, no shares may be available to borrow, so you must buy shares at whatever price they are trading—this is what Hal had to do.

Hal had to cover his short at $8.50 per share and ended up losing $360,000 on this trade. If Hal had done his due diligence after his initial investment paid off, swallowed his pride, and ceased and desisted from his shorting strategy, he would have made $30,000.

WHAT YOU SHOULD DO IF YOU'RE IN HAL'S PLACE

I'm not going to suggest you avoid complex or unusual investing techniques. You should, however, be sure that your pride is not obscuring the risks of these techniques. Admittedly, this is not always easy to do in the heat of the moment. Like Hal, you may feel you've come upon the perfect investing approach for a given time and market. It feels like an epiphany, and you are so excited about it you don't want to hear or read anything that diminishes your excitement. Therefore, you dismiss or rationalize whatever negatives accompany your approach. Hal didn't weigh the risks of a short-squeeze and failed to consider that, in shorting a stock, he faced potentially unlimited losses.

Risk-reward analysis is crucial here. Look at worst-case scenarios and calculate the odds that they might occur. Write down worst-case possibilities so you have them in black and white where they are more difficult to rationalize. Ask a professional for advice about the likelihood that they might occur with a given investment. Pride is strong, but it weakens when presented with evidence that a pride-based strategy is foolish.

Keep Your Pride in Check: Questions to Ask Yourself Prior to Making an Investment

If all this material suggests that you are an overly proud investor, your goal is to be aware of this tendency and manage it. It is unreasonable—not to mention highly unlikely—to expect that you will suddenly become a coldly rational, emotionally uninvolved investor. That is not who you are or who you should try to be. It is possible, though, to be proud of your investing knowledge and occasionally err in this direction without making some of the major mistakes we have discussed. The three steps suggested earlier will help you in this regard, and the following checklist will also help you monitor the tendency to invest for pride rather than for money:

__ Do you respond defensively when people ask you why you made a particular investment; do you find yourself vigorously or even angrily defending your position?

__ When someone offers you investing advice, do you frequently discount it; do you tell yourself that you know as much or more as the other person?

__ Are you likely to dismiss or not even look at investing newsletters, articles, and online sites, believing that anything that is in the public domain is for less knowledgeable investors?

__ Are you able to explain and support your investment rationale to others without boasting or making them feel inferior?

__ If you become aware of information that will negatively impact the price of a stock you recently purchased, are you willing to sell the stock, even at a loss?

__ Are you able to admit to friends, family, and colleagues that you invested in a loser or that your "brilliant" strategy was not so brilliant?

__ Are you willing to place money with an investment advisor or mutual fund manager who has an excellent track record?

__ Based on new information or a change in market conditions, are you willing to reverse your position and invest in a stock or fund that you previously declared was a poor investment?

Ask yourself these questions regularly and monitor the results. While you may not be able to place check marks next to all of them all the time, your goal should be to check off at least some of the questions.

Finally, here are some words to the wise that overly proud investors might want to frame and hang in any place where they regularly do their investing:

Your worth as a person is not determined by the worth of your portfolio.

You don't have to take every piece of advice you hear, but you do have to hear every piece of advice.

Don't confuse brains with a bull market.

Good investing means learning to admit you were wrong.

4

Lust

Losing Investing Perspective and Inhibitions

Lust may seem an odd term to describe an investing relationship, yet the characteristics of lust—obsessiveness, possessiveness, desire—are also traits that just about every investor has experienced. People fall head-over-heels in love with stocks that perform well. They become infatuated with strategies that they believe are foolproof. They lose their logic and operate strictly on emotion when they become obsessed with a certain fund.

In both love and investing, the problem with lust is that it feels like the real thing. Investors are convinced that they are making smart investing decisions when they are in lust. They are certain that their fierce loyalty to a stock or fund is justified, and that their heart is not getting in the way of their head.

In fact, lust prevents us from viewing our investing with logic and insight. We become so wrapped up in our investing obsession that we can't take that crucial step backwards and observe our investing self with any degree of objectivity. We don't benefit from hindsight or any other type of perspective; we can't say to ourselves, "That may have been a mistake."

At the same time, lusting after what seems like a terrific investment is only human. At some point, even the most objective and logical of us get taken for a ride by a hot stock. Fortunately, we can limit the damage if we maintain awareness of our vulnerability to lust. In addition, diversification provides an excellent hedge against inhibition-free, logic-free investing.

Lust can take different investing forms, and to give you a sense of the variety of ways it can affect you, let's look at three people who fell victim to this sin.

Three Lusty Losers

Jessica is a real estate broker who has been investing in KB Homes (KBH), a home builder since 2001. Because she knows the real estate sector well, she spotted KB as a winner almost from the start. She put in $15,000 when KB was just under $20 a share, and by 2005 it rose to $110; her investment was worth over $100,000. Combined with a number of dividend increases, Jessica has been amply rewarded by her initial investment. As a result, she has never sold a share of the stock. This is the best investment she has ever made, and she is convinced that KB will continue its upward trend for years. Jessica believes that the company's CEO is the best in the industry; she is certain that KB's strategy is light years ahead of competitors. She cannot see a weakness in the company, and in her mind, it is as sure a thing as exists in the market.

After watching the stock move steadily upward over the course of four years, Jessica liquidates her mutual fund holdings in her IRA and purchases another $75,000 of KB and then cashes in $13,000 of U.S. savings bonds, paying deferred taxes on the bonds in order to increase her stake in KB. Jessica does not view these actions as risky or foolish. In fact, she thinks she was being conservative by waiting so long to make these moves. She realizes that putting the majority of her money in one stock is not the best investing strategy, but she truly believes that KB is an exception to the rule. Every other investment she has made has gone up and down; KB has done nothing but go up. In fact, Jessica told a friend that if she could free up more money to invest in KB, she would do so in a second.

Invariably, Jessica will be burned by her strategy. Though as of this writing the stock has not gone down, it will likely descend at some point. While there is nothing wrong with her maintaining a large investment in KB, to have the majority of her net worth in one stock is irresponsible. If Jessica had any perspective, she would understand that the real estate industry has just completed a decade of phenomenal growth; that signs already exist that this growth is starting to slow; that rising interest rates will put the brakes on this growth; that other real estate stocks besides KB have done well over the last ten years, and that all of them will do poorly when the slowdown occurs. Jessica knows her industry and certainly is aware of the dramatic swings it experiences. Jessica, though, is convinced that KB is an exception to the rule. Her lust has blinded her to the realities of her industry, and sooner or later, she will pay for this sin.

Like Jessica, Al also turned an investment into the object of his lust. Unlike Jessica, he has already paid for this mistake. Al's lustful behavior began innocently enough. A lawyer who dabbled in the market, Al took a position in a small cap mutual fund in 1998. The ING Small Cap Opportunities Fund (NSPAX) specialized in finding small companies with good growth prospects. His initial $75,000 investment more than doubled over the next few years.

Al's rationale for holding onto this investment was purely emotional. Intellectually, Al recognized that small caps can be volatile, and that even though they had experienced greater growth in the late 1990s than bigger companies, they could sink as fast as they rose. He was so enamored of the fund's performance, though, that he rationalized the volatility; he told himself that the winners in the current market were those who had the fortitude to ride the volatility and then come out on top. If Al had been thinking clearly—if he had put his lawyer's logic to good use—he would have seen the flaw in his reasoning. He was convinced, though, that he had lucked into the fund of a lifetime. This is a common trait of lustful

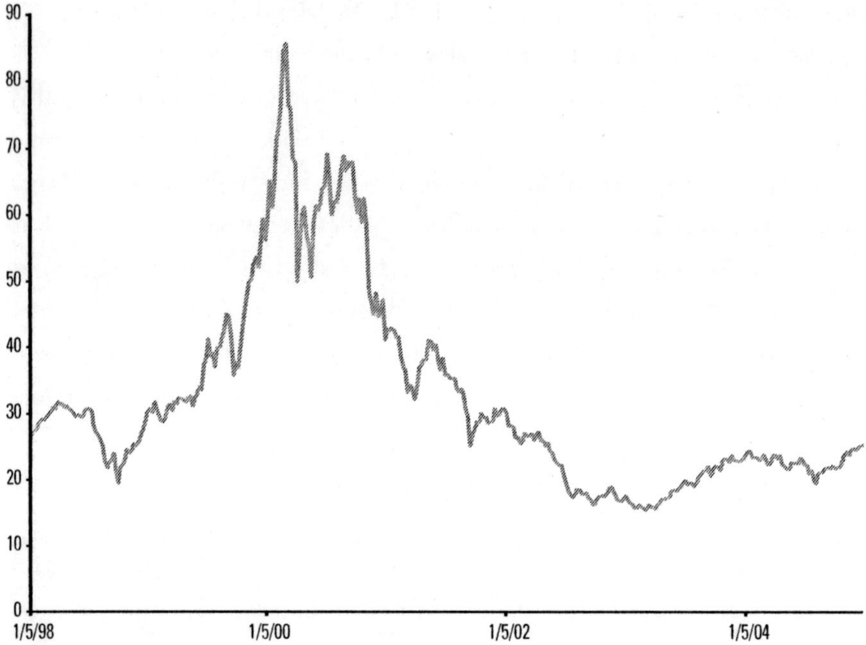

ING Small Cap Opportunities Fund: 1998–2004

investors: The belief that fate has smiled on them and handed them an opportunity that comes along once in a blue moon. For this reason, Al divested himself of equity and bond funds, putting as much money as he could into the ING Small Cap Fund.

By 2005, his portfolio was worth less than his total investment over the previous seven years. Eventually, he sold the fund at a loss and put most of the money into a short-term municipal fund yielding 2.6 percent. Like many sinful investors, Al's reaction to one sin led to another. He became slothful, parking his money in an overly safe vehicle and not even bothering to look at his statements. Like a jilted lover, Al shut down, unwilling to be jilted again.

Casey, a senior executive at a printing company, has avoided investing in equities since 1988. Instead, he is infatuated with his conservative approach. Over the years—especially in down markets—Casey has been ecstatic about his investments in intermediate (3 to 10 year) municipal bonds. After the tech bubble burst, Casey was obsessed with finding the most conservative vehicles for his money.

The fact that he has managed to earn just a bit more than inflation doesn't bother Casey; he lusts after conservative investments because he is convinced they prevent him from losing most or all of his hard-earned money. He relishes the tax-free income he receives from bonds and conveniently overlooks that he has never taken advantage of the 15 percent tax rate on dividend-paying stocks. When the cut in the dividend tax rate occurred and corporate America began increasing payouts to shareholders, Casey was oblivious. As companies such as Wal-Mart, Chevron, and Citigroup increased their dividends by more than 25 percent in the two years following the 2003 cut, Casey rationalized away the potential benefit to his portfolio. He also failed to consider that unlike bond yields, dividends can be increased and are rarely cut. The average dividend of the S&P 500 increased 11 percent. His conservative strategy made him feel secure and comfortable as an investor; that it was a false comfort didn't matter to Casey. In his mind, he was protecting himself from the inevitable market declines. He could even look at a statistic such as the 35 percent increase in energy stocks in 2005 and remain in lust with his strategy.

Thus, lust is a sin to which even conservative investors are vulnerable. Be aware, too, that it can manifest itself as an obsession with a strategy rather than with a particular stock or fund.

Types of Lust

As illustrated by the three previous stories, the following types of investing lust pose a danger to your portfolio:

- Holding on to a beloved investment much too long.
- Becoming infatuated with an investment's surface looks and buying too soon.
- Developing an obsession with Plain Jane investments.

Holding on to a Beloved Investment Much Too Long

This type of lust begins well but ends badly. Typically, you make an investment and it pays off handsomely. Over a period of time—usually weeks or months—it is a stellar performer. In many instances, it is the best investment you ever made. As the money rolls in, as your friends praise your foresight and as the pundits opine that this is a great stock or fund, you are helplessly in love. You reach a point when you are convinced that this will go on forever . . . or at least for a good long while. Even when evidence starts trickling in that selling would be a wise decision, you come up with ten reasons not to. You tell yourself that you don't want to pay capital gains taxes or that only fools and cowards would "betray" an investment that has done so well.

Consider the tremendous lust people felt for a stock such as WorldCom. A dollar invested in WorldCom at the beginning of the 1990s was worth $20 by the end of the decade. In July, 1999, its market capitalization was $180 billion. Three years later, WorldCom was bankrupt and the stock was worthless.

Did people hold on to WorldCom too long? Of course. Some people, though, were able to sell it before it made a huge dent in their portfolios. There was plenty of warning that some fuzzy accounting was going on, that instead of expensing certain items they were capitalizing them on the books, creating the illusion of profit instead of the reality of loss. Lust, though, caused some investors to hold on to the stock past all reason. Look at the performance of WorldCom stock on the opposite page.

Certainly at some point before the very end, investors had the opportunity to get out. Not only did many of them refuse to do so despite clear evidence that they should, but a significant percentage of WorldCom employees placed their entire 401(k) in the company stock. In 1999, WorldCom's success fostered the illusion that it was a superstock. In that year, WorldCom was worth more than Disney, Boeing, Walgreens, and Gillette combined.

All of us (myself included) fall in love with a good investment and hold it for a long time. That's fine. When love turns to lust, though, we invest too much of our portfolio and hold on to this investment past the time when all clear-thinking people would have sold some of it.

WorldCom: 1995–2002

If this particular type of lust sounds like it fits you, try the following to moderate its negative impact on your investing:

- Ask yourself how your financial position would be affected if the unthinkable happens: How much would you be hurt if the stock or fund that has you in its grip were to suddenly lose half its value? If it hurts just thinking about this possibility, you need to reduce your holding so the pain will be tolerable.
- Try selling a tiny amount of your lustful investment and invest the money in something completely different. Though you may feel like you're "betraying" your beloved investment and that you're a coward for doing so, this small act will help you start putting your investments in perspective. While people often have trouble selling a lot at once, a small reduction in their holding is an easier first step.

Another good way to moderate the impact of lust is to study the performance of other classic blue chip stocks such as Wal-Mart, Eastman Kodak, and Fifth Third Bank. As you can see from the accompanying charts on these pages, even these stocks that have inspired lust in millions have also performed in ways that broke people's hearts.

Becoming Infatuated with an Investment's Surface Looks and Buying Too Soon

Here the problem is lusting after a given investment even before it has proven its worth. For many reasons, people get it in their heads that a stock or fund is going to take off, and they buy too much too quickly. It is like falling in love at first sight. Suddenly, they have a singular focus and ignore everyone and every thing besides this one object of lust.

For instance, you subscribe to an investment newsletter, and you swear by it. In recent months, it has been right on the money with its

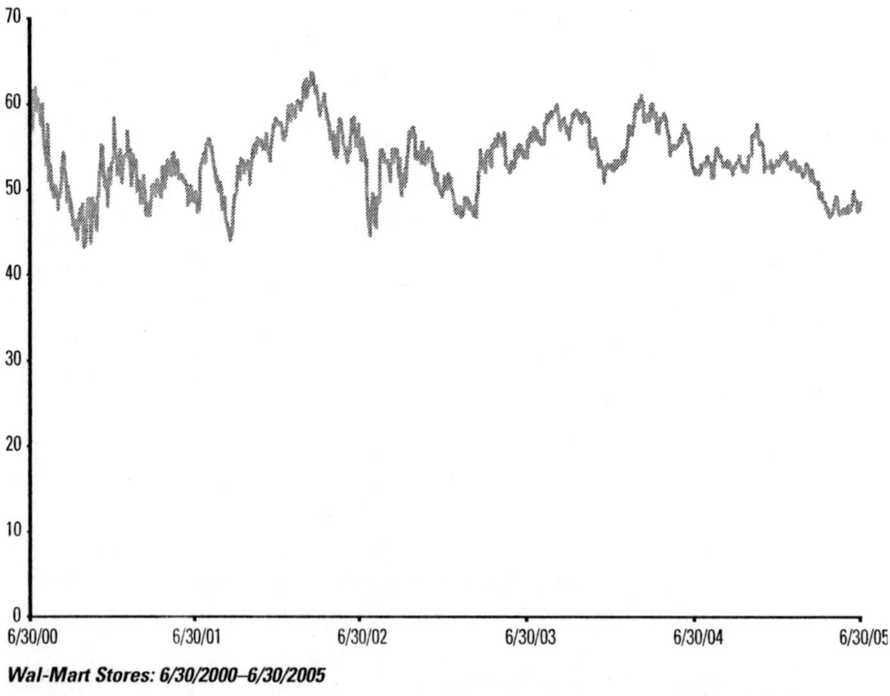

Wal-Mart Stores: 6/30/2000–6/30/2005

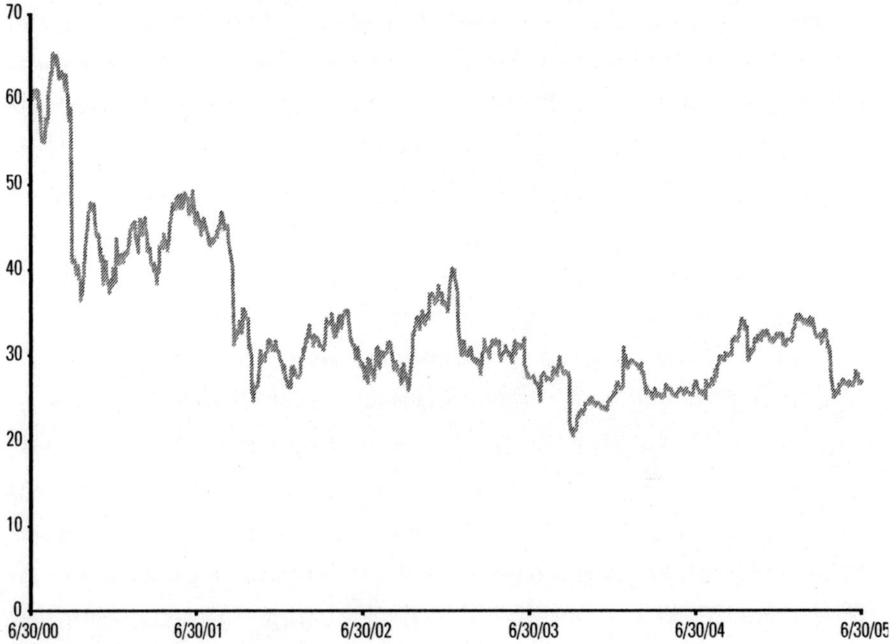

Eastman Kodak: 6/30/2000–6/30/2005

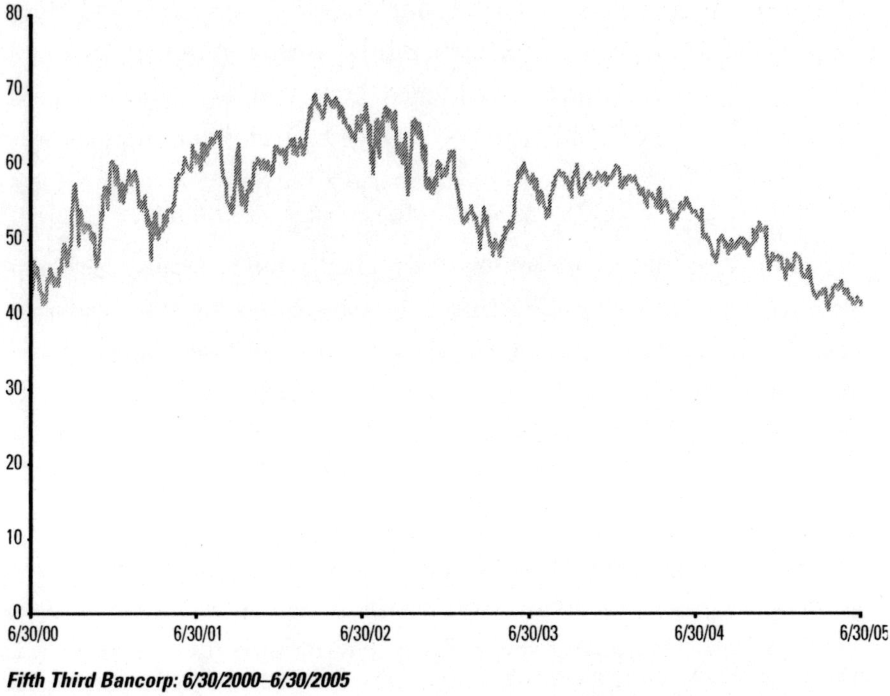

Fifth Third Bancorp: 6/30/2000–6/30/2005

recommendations, and it seems as if the newsletter author has the inside track on the market. Perhaps you recall George Gilder and his *Gilder Technology Report*. People made a great deal of money in the late 1990s investing in the tech companies Gilder recommended. In fact, his picks were like self-fulfilling prophecies: If George picked it, the stock would invariably rise. Of course, by late 2000 just about all the tech stocks went down and people who took Gilder's recommendations as gospel lost a lot of money.

Because Gilder was golden, lustful investors simply responded to his picks rather than doing their own due diligence. It is always a mistake to remove yourself entirely from the investment process. Whether you're relying on a newsletter or a stockbroker, you need to remain informed and involved. Unfortunately, lust seems to make that information and involvement irrelevant. When you have a worshipful faith in an individual or an investment, you lack the motivation to do your homework. As a result, you buy without adequate analysis and then end up holding on to an investment without adequate monitoring.

This leap-before-you-look syndrome can also involve a mutual fund. People have a tendency to lust after single-sector funds. If you had bought a biotech fund at the beginning of 2001, you would have suffered greatly. Over the next four years the average biotech fund dropped over 30 percent in value. During this same period, the S&P 500 dropped less than 2 percent.

Similarly, people become obsessed with hedge funds because they help them win while everyone else seems to be losing. Some investors confer an exalted status on these funds and invest in them based only on the fact that they returned 15 percent in the previous year, unaware that they plunged 25 percent two years before. It is astonishing that many hedge fund investors don't realize that these funds are loosely regulated partnerships that may invest in illiquid or nonmarketable securities. They can be extremely volatile and carry a high degree of risk. They are appropriate investments for a small part of your portfolio, but should never become your primary investment vehicle. Every few months there is an article about some hedge fund closing its doors and returning nothing to its investors. While such an event is very rare, inevitably there are investors who put all their net worth in one of these funds. In most cases when nothing is returned there is fraud involved. Anyone who has studied hedge funds over time recognizes that if retirement is your primary goal, it is a mistake to put a significant percentage of your portfolio in them.

To avoid this type of lust, do the following:

- Tell yourself that gurus and their newsletters are fallible, and that it's fine to listen to their advice but you still must be responsible for research and analysis. Don't worship gurus. Instead, respect them but vet their picks through your own evaluation process.
- Count to ten before you buy. Not ten seconds, but ten days or even ten weeks. Give yourself enough time to observe how a given stock or fund performs and get a sense of why it performs the way it does. Obviously, you don't want to wait too long and miss out on a good deal, but it is much wiser to invest with your head than your heart. The former takes longer—any analysis of data is a relatively lengthy process—but it protects you from your own impulsiveness.
- Be cautious around single-sector funds, especially those that have enjoyed significant success over a period of months or years. As attractive as their returns might be, you are likely too late to the game, and at best you'll catch the tail end of the cycle before you start losing big-time.
- Do not invest more than 5 percent of your net worth in a single volatile, speculative fund (such as a hedge fund).

Developing an Obsession with Plain Jane Investments

Lusting after unattractive people may seem counterintuitive, but it happens all the time. In investing, this behavior may happen on the rebound: You've been burned by a volatile stock once too often. Whatever the reason, you gravitate toward the safest investments you can find. When the market falls, you feel even closer to your conservative investing strategy than you did before.

The problem, of course, is that safe investments foster an illusion of wisdom. You love the strategy because you're protected from loss and because you know that your small gains each year will eventually add up to a significant amount. In down markets, especially, you are enraptured by how well you do compared with how poorly others fare.

To shatter the illusion, consider the investor who has been crowing about his tax-free money market account for the first half of the decade. This investor would have a total cumulative return of 7.4 percent for this period. Shockingly, merely to keep up with the rate of inflation over these five years, this investor would have had to earn a total return of 11.3 percent.

There's nothing wrong with having some money in these safe investments. To avoid the market entirely, however, is often a result of lustful thinking. The individual who is so in love with his ultra-conservative strategy can talk himself into avoiding a declining or volatile market entirely. Why take the risk of being caught in the downslide? If this investor were thinking clearly, however, he would realize that opportunities exist to invest in the S&P 500 at attractive levels even when a market has been in decline. In the last five years, for instance, the S&P 500 was as low as 800, but by 2005 it was up to 1,275. If our hypothetical investor had taken 20 percent of his cash out of his money market funds and bought the S&P Index at 800 in late 2002, his 7.4 percent return for the five-year period would have increased to 17 percent for the entire portfolio.

Keep in mind, therefore, that even the safest investment is not safe from inflation. I know of no better way of keeping lustful investors away from ultra-conservative strategies than to cite the Ibbotson and Associates study of the market between 1925 and 2004. During this period, large company stocks returned 10.4 percent per year on average. If you were to have missed being in the market for only 38 months out of the total 948 months, your return would drop to just 4.5 percent annually for the 79-year period. Similarly, if you missed the best 19 months between 1984 and 2004, your return would be only around 3.5 percent rather than 13 percent annual return that everyone who stayed in the market received.

Why Lust Happens

As you're reading this, you may think to yourself, "I'm never going to commit this sin." Everyone thinks this thought. When you're reading about other people, their lustful investing behavior seems completely irrational. In the heat of investment decision-making, however, lust can hit you when you least expect it. Certain situations present themselves and rational thought takes a back seat to the moment's infatuation. It pays, therefore, to be alert for the following situations where you're most vulnerable to lustful investing:

BUYING STOCK IN YOUR OWN COMPANY

There are all sorts of direct and indirect messages that make you feel your company stock is going to perform better than any other stock. You observe that your organization is extremely well-managed, that the company has great products and services and that its leaders are inspirational and honest. As our WorldCom example illustrated, it is not unusual for people to invest their entire retirement funds in their own company stock. You may receive stock options and other incentives to buy the company stock, and your boss or some other executive may assure you that it's the best investment you could possibly make. In some cases, management may apply pressure for you to invest in the company and they may monitor your equity holdings. For some people, it feels disloyal to invest in any other company's stock.

If this describes your investing, I don't want to suggest that you've been brainwashed, but you certainly have been smitten. Why else would you entrust your livelihood and your life savings to one company? As great as your company's management may be, people change companies. As wonderful as your company's products are, new products with new technologies render established products obsolete.

It's fine to invest in your company, but if possible limit that investment to no more than 10 percent of your net worth.

A SECTOR TAKES OFF, AND YOU TAKE OFF WITH IT

People become sector crazed. I cannot tell you the number of people who became tech-sector fanatics. Individuals who can avoid lusting after a single stock or fund lose all perspective when it comes to sectors. Whether its technology, energy, or emerging market stocks, some sector seems to be "it." Investors are always looking for the magic bullet, and sectors seem to create the illusion of magic better than other investing strategies. A hot sector seems like it's going to be hot forever; it seems to have tapped into a larger societal trend and therefore won't disappear any time soon.

While sectors may have more staying power than an individual stock, they too have their ups and downs. Although one of the great benefits of investing in a sector is that you achieve a degree of diversification, you can still lose a great deal of money. To reduce the chances of this happening, make sure that you don't have a large percentage of your portfolio devoted to only one part of the market.

WORSHIPING THE FUND GURUS

Some of the managers of major funds have become celebrities. Some of them deserve their fame; they enjoy excellent track records. Nonetheless, investors become so wrapped up in their infallibility that they follow their recommendations to the letter. In other words, they stop thinking for themselves. This can be very dangerous, especially when a fund guru becomes infatuated with himself and stops thinking clearly. Some gurus, too, can make recommendations more for publicity than for any other purpose.

If you follow a guru's advice, take it with a grain of salt and be sure to do your own homework to confirm that his recommendations make sense.

THE FRENZY TRAP

Over the years, I have seen certain stocks deified: Cisco, Amazon.com, Kohl's, and Coca-Cola. The company performance is through the roof, everyone is recommending that you buy, and the stock takes on an aura that is nigh irresistible.

Resist. If you get caught up in the frenzy, you lose all perspective. As a general rule, when the frenzy reaches the point that not only you but your neighbor and your brother-in-law are all lusting after a certain stock, you probably have missed out on your best opportunity to invest.

INVESTING IN THE CEO

We live in an age of celebrity CEOs such as Steve Jobs and Bill Gates. After reading their books, seeing their interviews, and hearing analysts praise them to the skies, it's a surprise that more people don't lust after their company stocks. As important as CEOs are to a company's success, they are only one of many factors. Even the best CEOs run into problems beyond their control. CEOs who have been considered terrific leaders have been felled by foreign competition, a competitor's innovative new technology, and other events. Wise investors may think a CEO walks on water, but they invest in more than the magic and mystique of one leader. They ask the hard questions about the company, its financial performance, its competitive situation, and so on. If it's a tie between a CEO you worship and a financial report that is so-so, the tie goes to the financial report.

A cautionary tale for all investors who lust after CEOs involves Al Dunlap, the former CEO of Sunbeam. He was considered a brilliant turnaround artist who had done wonders at Scott Paper and was hired by Sunbeam in 1996 to resurrect the company. Amid much positive publicity, Dunlap began "trimming the fat," a cost-cutting trait that earned him the name "Chainsaw Al." This time, though, it didn't work. In fact, Dunlap was fired in 1998 in a cloud of controversy involving improper accounting, sagging sales, and an outrageous compensation package. In Dunlap's two years as CEO, the stock dropped 65 percent from its high. In 2001, Sunbeam filed for bankruptcy.

THE PERFECT PRODUCT

You drive a Cadillac and love GM; you own an iPod and think Apple is the greatest company ever to have been founded. If you rely on your personal passion for a product or service to guide your investing, your strategy is fundamentally flawed. When it comes to investing, you can't trust your own experiences. They are too narrow to be generalized to the company's financial performance. Admittedly, it's human nature to generalize personal experience, especially when you have such strong feelings for a product. If your father always drove a Cadillac and you've always driven one, it stands to reason that you assume GM makes great products and that it will always do well.

In reality, the underlying fundamentals are what you need to investigate. Sometimes great products have poor profit margins. Sometimes great services will soon be eclipsed by companies with greater services. It may be that a product or service is truly superior, but you're investing too late to take advantage of a reasonable stock price.

I love XM Satellite Radio, but I would not buy the stock now. If I had discovered it early, it might have been a worthwhile investment. Too many people have jumped on the bandwagon, and all the bandwagon jumpers and good news about its potential are reflected in the high price. It's a terrific product, but after looking at the prospective competitors, the subscription rate, and the rising technology costs, I realized that my personal enthusiasm for the product was not matched by my professional enthusiasm for the stock.

Diversification: Spread Your Love Around

Everyone talks about having a diversified portfolio but few do much about it. As much as we may admire the concept of diversification intellectually, our investing often doesn't put this concept into practice. That's because we're lustful. We become fixated on one type of stock or sector of the marketplace and put all or most of our eggs in one basket. As I noted earlier, diversification is a hedge against lustful investing. To diversify, however, you need to understand more than the surface argument in its favor. First, let me explain why it's such an effective strategy today, especially if you are vulnerable to lustful investing behaviors. Second, I'll suggest some ways to diversify your portfolio that do an excellent job of countering your lustful tendencies.

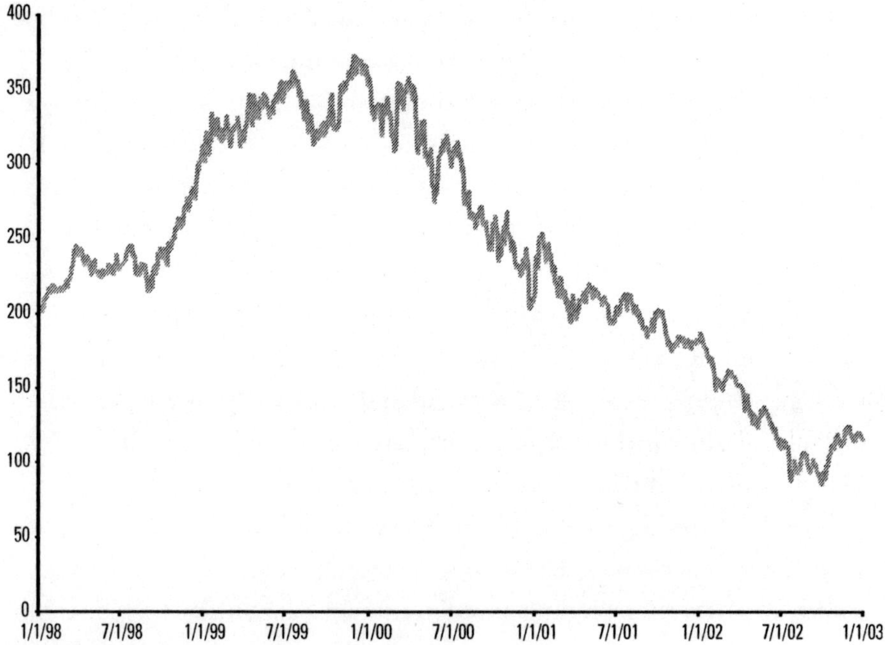

Dow Jones US Total Market Telecommunications Index: 1998–2002

More so than ever before, people are investing in particular industries, attempting to spot the hot ones early and ride the rise in the market. This would be fine if you could get in early, ride the rise, and know when to jump off. The lustful investor, though, tends to jump in a bit too late and hold on too long. When a portfolio is heavily weighted toward one industry, it is vulnerable to volatility and long-term change in investor sentiment to that industry. All it takes is a lack of earnings growth or a macro change in the industry's prospects for investor sentiment to turn south.

Consider the telecommunications industry. In the late 1990s, a tremendous demand for Internet pipeline existed. The telecommunications industry expanded capacity to meet this demand the market pushed up the prices of all the companies involved, including Verizon, Sprint, and Level 3.

When the market realized that Internet demand was not going to grow at 50 percent per quarter indefinitely, company share prices fell by 50 to

70 percent. Stocks in this sector traded at lower prices than when they had traded seven years before in late 1998 prior to the massive tech rally.

What if your lustful behavior had caused you to invest the majority of your portfolio in telecommunications stocks? You would have been up the creek without a paddle. You would have lacked a hedge against inflation and your retirement fund would have diminished at an alarming rate.

Diversification over a range of companies and industries, though, often seems like an indecisive strategy to some investors. They would prefer to invest boldly, to go with their instincts and their passions. Years ago, this strategy was probably more effective than it is today. We live in an unpredictable, volatile world, and unless you are truly diversified, you are likely to be burned. All it takes is an unexpected slowdown in a company's business, not controlling expenses or missing earnings targets and a golden investment can become fool's gold seemingly overnight. More significantly, legal issues including fraud routinely take stocks that investors lusted after and turn them into ones the market shuns. Enron, WorldCom,

Crown Holdings: 1998–2001

and HealthSouth are just a few examples of companies whose fraudulent activities were difficult for any investor to foresee. Lawsuits involving everything from stock manipulation to environmental offenses have brought a number of major companies to their knees. While most people are aware of the litigation against tobacco companies, they may not be aware that solid companies such as Owens Corning, Armstrong World, and W.R. Grace sought bankruptcy protection to deal with lawsuits.

As an investor, therefore, you may believe that a given company is as good as a company gets, but if you place the majority of your investing money in its stock, you stand a good chance of regretting it. Consider Crown Holdings, Inc. (CCK), a leading manufacturer of beverage and food cans. Crown Holdings was well-managed, highly profitable, and enjoyed a great reputation. It attracted many prudent investors who thought they had found the ideal stock. In 1963 Crown Holdings bought an insulation business that made a product alleged to contain asbestos. They sold this business three months after purchasing it. The asbestos scare about thirty-five years later drove the stock price of Crown Holdings down from the $40s range to $1 in 2001. Astonishingly and unpredictably, a seemingly insignificant event from the distant past made a good investment a lousy one.

The days of blue chip stocks performing consistently and predictably well over a long period of time are over. Who knew that 9/11 and ill-timed expansion would drive UAL into bankruptcy? Conseco, a highly recommended insurance company, overpaid for acquisitions, took on too much debt, and careened into bankruptcy. Kmart was praised by many and its performance was stellar until Wal-Mart beat them at their own game and Kmart was saddled with dozens of leases on stores that never were profitable; they too went into bankruptcy.

Forgive this diatribe on the volatility and uncertainty that govern company fortunes today, but I want to impress upon you the dangers of lusting after stocks that can turn on you faster than you might think. People frequently underestimate this volatility or take the attitude that "it can't happen to my stock." It can and will. Diversification will protect you from your myopia. Let's look at the best ways to diversify as an investor.

Some experts will advise that diversification means owning five different stocks. Others will advocate spreading your portfolio over the S&P 500. I'm not going to recommend a specific number; I'm going to provide an effective diversification strategy that counters the sin of lust. Here are the steps I recommend:

1. Consider using Exchange Traded Funds (ETFs) for instant diversification. A product that debuted in the late 1990s, ETFs are liquid and tax-efficient, and best of all, they immediately counter the impulse to fall madly in love with one stock. If you want to buy the energy market, for instance, you can purchase the Energy Select Sector Index Fund (XLE). SPDR (pronounced spyder) is the brand-name fund sponsor State Street Bank has given this product. The Energy ETF trades daily on the American Stock Exchange and consists of all the large U.S.–based oil and energy companies—twenty-nine in all, weighted by market capitalization—and includes 20 percent invested in Exxon-Mobil, 14 percent in Chevron Texaco, and 8 percent in Conoco Phillips. The underlying management fee of the fund is a modest .24 percent per annum. The ETF pays a dividend just like a normal stock and also has a mechanism that limits the amount of capital gains that are declared, thus saving taxes for investors.

2. When selecting individual stocks, keep your positions between 2 and 3 percent. In a portfolio of 60 percent equities, for example, you might have 20 to 30 positions according to this formula. No doubt, good selections will naturally grow beyond 3 percent, but you should cut back as soon as they move above the 5 percent ceiling. Remember, your tendency will be to treat your winners like a favored child, but if you allow your winners to dominate your portfolio, you'll get hurt in a market sell-off.

3. To make sure you diversify your industries as well as your individual stocks, never place more than one-quarter of your equity portfolio in any single industry. No doubt, you have sector biases. I do too—I'm generally most comfortable with banks and insurance. You can indulge these biases to a certain extent, but when you hit the 25 percent mark, yellow lights should start flashing in your head. Keep in mind the fate that befalls sector-lusting investors: They are overexposed in a sector that is losing value while the balance of the market is appreciating.

4. Be an opportunistic seller of company stock. One of the objections lustful investors raise when I talk about not falling in love with their company stock is that there are so many powerful incentives to accumulate this stock. Not only do some employees receive stock as part of their compensation package, but the stock does not always vest until five years later and cannot be sold until it is vested. In addition, companies offer 401(k) and retirement plans and employees often feel direct and indirect pressure to put some or all of their monies in these plans.

Therefore, sell company stock when you have the chance and the market is right. Try as assiduously as you can to keep your company stock at 10 percent or less of your portfolio.

5. Resist the temptation to shift a significant amount of your diversified portfolio into a single investment. In other words, even if you have achieved your diversification goal, you're not necessarily fully protected against becoming infatuated with a stock or narrowly assembled fund. More often than not, this infatuation strikes suddenly and without warning. You read in a newsletter how people are making fortunes in semiconductors and you're sitting there earning a reasonable but unspectacular return. The more you read about semiconductors, the more in love you fall. Before you know it, you're switching 30 percent of your holdings into semiconductors. If you do well initially, you may put another 20 percent in. Then the bottom falls out and you experience the agony of being spurned by the stock you loved. If you feel compelled to shift some money out of your diversified portfolio, limit the shift to no more than 5 percent.

If these five "rules" seem to reflect a doomsday mentality, remember that you're not playing the slots in Vegas. If you're like most investors, you are investing for a major future goal and not to get rich quick. Given this goal, you need to take out some insurance, protecting yourself from slot machine players who pull the lever with an obsessiveness that only relents when all their money is gone. These rules are your insurance, safeguarding your investments against your all-too-human impulses.

5

Avarice

Even King Midas Didn't Have the Touch

Greed is a tricky subject when it comes to investing since the point of this activity is to make money. From a sin-based perspective, however, investors cross the line when they desire to make too much money too fast; when in their rush to make piles of money, they forget to do their homework and their expectations are wildly out of line with reality. Driven by greed, investors tend to jump on bandwagons too late and stay on too long, or they invest heavily in a stock that on the surface looks like a winner but quickly turns into a loser. They invest dreaming of riches, and these dreams distort their reasoning.

All of this is not to suggest that wanting to make money through investing is a sin. There is nothing greedy about keeping ahead of inflation and taking advantage of the dividends that comes with equity investing. To park all your funds in the money market ignores economic realities. For instance, if you invested your money in a bank or money market fund or treasury bills between 1995 and 2005, you would have earned approximately 3.75 percent. Paying income tax on the earnings would have reduced this to less than 2.8 percent. The inflation rate for this period was a low 2.5 percent, giving you a net real return of only .3 percent. In an ordinary period of inflation, you would have lost money. Therefore, don't label yourself as greedy just because you want to increase the worth of your portfolio.

Market conditions can also influence how greed is defined. In 2000 I asked a colleague if he would lock up a 10 percent tax-free return for the rest of his life on his portfolio. He looked at me as if I were crazy. Why would anyone settle for such a low return? Five years later my clients are praying for 7 to 8 percent returns over time. I mention this to warn you about fixing on a specific numerical financial goal as the line that divides the greedy from the nongreedy. This line can shift based on market conditions and many other factors.

If you want to see what a truly greedy investor looks like regardless of market conditions, though, let me introduce you to Lloyd.

Betting Too Much, Too Fast, on Too Little Evidence

In late 1999, people were looking for stocks with tremendous upside volatility. They pounced on any piece of news about these companies, anticipating that it would send the stock price shooting skyward. Lloyd, a client of mine, was this type of investor. On December 8, 1999, Lloyd saw a report on CNBC that AT&T had made an investment in Internet Capital Group (ICGE), an Internet holding company. ICGE was in the process of acquiring other companies that provided software and network solutions to corporate clients, and this seemed like the perfect investment to Lloyd. His logic was that if a blue chipper like AT&T would spend $50 million on this holding company, they must know something other people didn't. In addition, First Union Securities has rated ICGE a "strong buy" and placed a $150 price target on the stock. This was enough to convince Lloyd to buy 500 shares of ICGE at $85 per share. He had done very little research, but Lloyd, like a lot of people at the time, was convinced that the right tech investment was a ticket to a lifetime of leisure. Lloyd was amazed that more people weren't following his lead, but he had always believed that most investors were overly cautious and missed out on great deals because of their caution.

The following week after Lloyd bought the stock, Ford announced that they had purchased $50 million in ICGE stock. A week later, Alex Brown placed a $240 price target on the stock. By year end ICGE was worth $170 per share.

Lloyd was licking his chops, certain that the price would continue to soar. On January, 3, 2000, ICGE peaked at a closing price of $200 per share. The market capitalization stood at $6 billion. ICGE had gone public only three months earlier at $6 per share and marketing capitalization of $180 million. In three weeks, the investment had appreciated an astonishing 135 percent. Surely that would be enough to satisfy even the greediest of investors. I suggested to Lloyd that he sell some of the stock or some

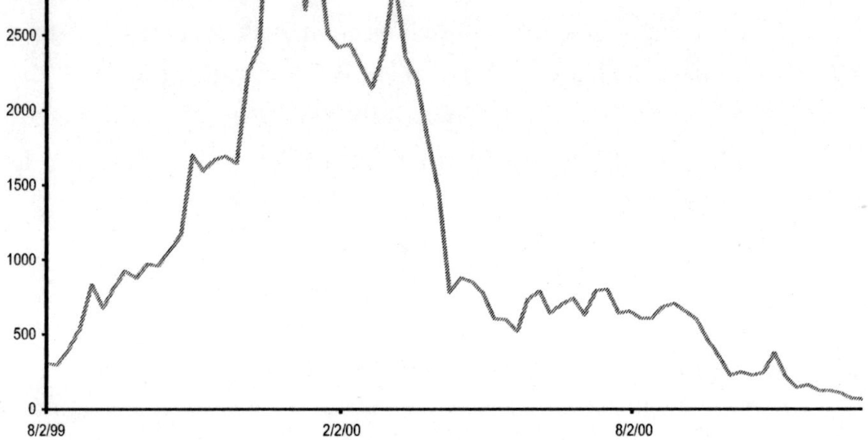

Internet Capital Group: 8/1/1999–12/31/2000

covered calls to lock in a portion of his gain. Lloyd acted like I had suggested he toss a suitcase of $100 bills into Lake Michigan.

After a few months, though, the market cooled and Lloyd considered selling as the price dropped to $120 per share. Lloyd, though, was too greedy; he continued to look for the uptrade, waiting for the stock to recover a bit before he sold. It never did. By March 31st, the price had gone below Lloyd's purchase price of $85. By May, the stock was down in the $20s. Still Lloyd held on, and as far I know, he's holding on still. ICGE is still around as of this writing, but after accounting for a 1 for 20 reverse stock split, it is trading at 27 cents a share. Lloyd's investment of $42,500 is worth $135. Perhaps he takes solace in the fact that AT&T's and Ford's investment of $50 million is worth only $160,000.

Lloyd's story is a cautionary tale for greedy investors, but it may be one that is difficult to heed. If you ever have seen the old Humphrey Bogart movie, T*he Treasure of Sierra Madre,* you know how greed can distort your thinking. In that movie, Bogart is one of three prospectors searching for gold. As their search brings them closer and closer to the gold, all of them change for the worse. Their camaraderie and decency dissolve. More significantly, their perspective becomes distorted. Bogart is literally driven mad by his greed.

I'm not suggesting that greedy investors are insane, though they routinely exhibit crazy investing behaviors. In some instances, such as the one just described, their initial decision-making may be sound. ICGE would have been a good investment if Lloyd had approached the investment knowledgeably and objectively. His greed, though, skewed his judgment. Two of the common failings of greedy investors are: 1) The lack of an investing plan and 2) The lack of research about the investment.

If Lloyd had had a plan, he might have decided to sell some or all of the stock when it reached a certain number. If he had done any research, he would have known that ICGE had already risen 1,300 percent in the four months before he bought the stock; he might have thought to himself, "What goes up that high must come down."

Greedy Investor versus Realistic Investor

Greedy investors are unrealistic in their expectations. As our earlier metaphor suggested, they operate under the same delusions as Las Vegas gamblers: They are convinced that with the right system and a little bit of luck, they will make a mint. No doubt, most investors hope to make a lot of money with their stock picks, but they temper that hope with realistic expectations. They expect to make a lot of money in the long run, not with one spin of the wheel.

Determining if you are committing the sin of greed in your investing, however, is not always easy. You may think to yourself, "I invested in Stock A because I was sure it was going to go through the roof. It didn't. Therefore, I was motivated by greed, and that was why I made a bad investment."

Not necessarily. We all have our moments when we make an investment because we anticipate a significant return, but it is one thing to base the investment on extensive research and another thing entirely to base it on one flimsy bit of evidence and a great deal of unrealistic expectations. For instance, I bought Allstate Insurance in 2000 at around $19 per share. Over the next few years, I was hoping for a significant return. My reasoning was that Allstate, one of the country's largest insurance companies, traded as high as $40 in 1998 and earned $3.08 per share. In 1999 Allstate earned $2.68. Wall Street hates to see this decline in earnings, though it was primarily due to Allstate reserving money for a large amount of storms in 1999. Most analysts expected Allstate earnings to drop further in 2000, and they in fact went down to $2.11 per share. Nonetheless, my rationale was that Allstate was an extremely large, historically successful company run by very savvy people, and that they would figure out a way to adjust pricing and get earnings back on track. Although I wasn't sure when this would happen, I was willing to wait since I owned the company at a valuation of nine times "depressed" earnings. Plus, I would be paid a 3.5 percent dividend while I waited for earnings improvement. In addition, I compared how companies similar to Allstate were trading on a price-to-earnings ratio—they were trading at PE ratios in excess of 12.

I believe that even if Allstate earnings remained where they were, the stock had a decent chance to rise to $25 per share to equal the PE of other leading insurance companies.

In 2001 Allstate earnings recovered to $3 per share. By 2005, they were up to near $6 per share and the stock was trading in the mid-50s. The point, though, is that I exhibited traits that greedy investors never exhibit: patience and due diligence. I didn't buy Allstate because of one news item I read in the paper, nor did I sink a huge amount of my portfolio into it. I did my homework, waited, and was rewarded, with a return on the investment substantially higher than the overall stock market.

I was a realistic investor, as opposed to a greedy investor. Which are you? The following comparative traits may help you decide:

Greedy Investor

1. Initial motivation to purchase is sparked by the likelihood of a big (50 percent or more) increase in the stock triggered by an event or news.

2. First question might be, "How quick will this work for me?"

3. Second question, "So how high do you think the stock could go?"

4. May spend only two minutes considering stock before buying.

5. Will likely hear about this stock from a friend, colleague, or barber. Most important due diligence may be to ask, "Who else bought the stock?"

6. After a successful purchase, the comment might be, "This stock has a lot more in! I am not selling till I double my money!"

7. As the stock is falling: "It sounded like a good idea at the time. I guess it was too good to be true."

8. When it's time to sell: "So Frank sold his stock and Jenny sold hers, well I guess this is the time for me to sell. And to think I could have sold this 'pig' at a profit and not have taken a bath with it!"

Realistic Investor

1. This person may be initially driven to a stock because of attractive valuation versus competitors or other sectors.
2. First question might be, "What is a likely timeframe for this company to improve earnings or repair its balance sheet?"
3. Second question might be, "What are the company's earnings and dividend and is the dividend at risk for a cut or might it increase?"
4. May spend an hour looking at earnings reports and comparing this company to others in the same industry.
5. Will probably learn about the company from reading a business periodical or a story on the Internet and will care little if others have bought the stock.
6. After a successful purchase: "How does this company's valuation compare now to the market, and its competitors? Are the prospects for further appreciation still reasonable?"
7. As the market is falling: "I will be able to ride this out. The earnings are improving and they just raised the dividend. When the market improves this stock will perform much better."
8. When it's time to sell: "Now that I have held this long enough to qualify for capital gains treatment and the company is trading at a PE that is higher than the competition, and I see more attractive stocks in the market, I will sell."

Recognizing When Greed Is Causing Your Investing Problems

It may be that as you look at the previous section and clearly identify yourself as a greedy rather than as a realistic investor, your response is, "So what?" You may rationalize this investing behavior as crucial to your success. You are aggressive, confident, and willing to take risks; you made a significant amount of money in the market in the past, and you intend to do so in the future, and the only way you know how to do so is by thinking big and investing like a big-time player.

In fact, big-time investors are big-time precisely because they aren't greedy. They are highly successful because they understand the way the market works, do their homework, analyze their options carefully, and then make decisions with both short-term and long-term results in mind. The greedy investor, on the other hand, gets into all sorts of financial trouble because his greed is based on an unrealistic view of the market.

For instance, greedy investors frequently fire their financial advisors for the worst reasons. The only thing that might be keeping their portfolios healthy is taking at least some good advice from investment advisors, and once they end these relationships, their portfolios suffer. Typically, the greedy investor will be at a cocktail party, work, or some other function and someone will be talking about how his money manager helped him secure a return of 20 percent in the year just ended. The greedy investor, who only had a 10 percent return, will immediately fire his advisor for only performing half as effectively as this other person's money manager. While it may be true that this money manager did a great job this year, the question that is rarely asked is: "How did this person do the year before, and the year before that?" It may be that in the previous year, this money manager lost 20 percent while the market was only down 5 percent. The point is that you need to be thorough and analytical about all your investing decisions, and greed can cause you to act reflexively and emotionally.

Greed also causes people to chase performance. They focus on finding the hot money manager or mutual fund, as if this discovery might be the magic they need to find their pot of gold. The problem with focusing on a person or investment who will make you rich is twofold: Not only do you ignore the investments and advice that will make you wealthy in the long-term, but you are blind to how this greedy investment strategy sets you up for a fall. For instance, greedy investors pile into energy stocks after they have appreciated 40 percent the previous year, failing to realize that the odds of this trend continuing are considerably reduced by the previous year's unprecedented success. Or they dump their underperforming drug stocks when they are at decade-low prices, failing to assess whether there is a reasonable chance that they have hit bottom and will start a slow but steady climb from this point forward. Or they avoid stable, large-capitalization stocks that may only appreciate at 10 to 15 percent annually since in their mind, this is only average performance.

This desire for high performance makes them vulnerable to being burned. They place too much value on any tip that crosses their paths, regardless of the source. If their barber, best friend, or bartender gives them some "inside information" about a stock, they often take it as gospel because their greed makes them want it to be true. They may even artificially elevate a prospective investment in their own minds, convincing themselves that A plus B equals X; that a news report about a resurgence in the biotech market combined with a favorable university study about a new biotech product means they should invest heavily in a biotech company that just went public.

The third negative outcome of greed is a lack of due diligence. In their rush to strike it rich, investors make decisions based on scant research. When considering various options, they don't compare the revenues, PE ratio, or measures for the peer group. They aren't aware of cash flow needs of the relevant companies or earnings growth (or lack thereof) over a period of time. What they usually do know is a single, overwhelming fact that (in their minds) makes everything else superfluous. Here are some examples of overwhelming facts:

- A new "superstar" CEO has been named to head a company, and he enjoyed spectacular success at the previous company he headed, as described in a cover article in a major business publication.
- The stock price is rising rapidly on the basis of rumors about the company's R&D breakthrough.
- A friend who has a brother-in-law who works for an organization told you that his brother-in-law's company will be making

an announcement next week that it is merging with its biggest competitor.

- You were watching the news and your favorite stock analyst enthusiastically and convincingly recommended a stock.

- You saw a list of the best performing mutual funds for last years, and the one at the top of the list has delivered an astonishing 32 percent.

These facts make greedy investors act before thinking. They are so concerned at missing out on a windfall, they buy before they have done the proper research. Though I'm not a psychologist, it seems reasonable to speculate that they don't want to do the research because it might dash their dreams of riches—the fund that delivered 32 percent in the past year may have recorded a minus 35 percent in the previous year.

In addition, greed often prevents investors from monitoring their successful investments for numerical and other signs that it's time to sell. Greedy investors always want more, and they have trouble admitting to themselves that a successful investment won't keep being successful indefinitely. Even after tripling their money and having a stock that is selling at 100 times earnings, greedy investors won't get rid of it; they won't even be aware of the multiple at which it's selling. They won't take the time to look at the investment from a historical perspective and put its present performance in context. As a result, they invariably push a successful investment's limit too far; they lack the data to identify when a stock price is at, near, or just past its apogee, and the only direction left is down. Even when it goes down, they don't study all the data about the stock, the events taking place in the company, market trends, and so on. Instead, they may seize on one piece of positive news and use it to convince themselves that a stock will return to its former glory. Thus, they hold on to a loser far too long and suffer more losses than less greedy investors.

Manage the Reflex: How to Keep Your Greed Under Control

Greed is one of the most difficult sins to manage because it is always there. We invest to make money, and every promising investment raises the possibility of making a significant amount of money. We wouldn't be human if part of us didn't dream a bit about what might be. Good investors, though, keep that part of themselves in a controlled, isolated environment. If you are particularly vulnerable to the sin of greed, you'll do likewise. Specifically, you'll do some or all of the following:

1. ***Invest slowly, knowledgably, and logically.*** Speed, ignorance, and reflex are the greedy investor's enemies. Force yourself to move relatively slowly before making an investing decision, even when you're certain that even a moment's delay could cost you thousands. In the vast majority of cases, delaying your decision for a short period of time won't hurt. In most instances, it helps because it gives you a bigger window of time in which you can think, reflect, learn, and talk about an investment. Greed preys on people who just react. When I say invest knowledgably, I mean do your homework. Learn about the fund's or stock's performance historically. Compare the fund or stock to the appropriate index or benchmark. Read as many reports as you can related to the investment. Don't worry that your delay makes you spend an extra 50 cents a share because in the long run it won't make a difference. Finally, logical investing means reasoning out your investment decision. When you hear a great tip or read something that makes you believe you've found a great fund that will make you millions, step back and write down the logical steps that have led you to this conclusion. Specifically:

- Analyze the source. Is the individual credible? What do you know about this individual? Is he a professional investment advisor? If so, what is his track record—do you know anything about how well his recommendations have panned out in the past?

- Assess your information depth. How much information have you gathered about the investment? A little? A moderate amount? A lot? Is the information from credible sources, and are their multiple pieces of information that support your conclusions?

- Figure out why you feel so compelled to make this investment. Try and take a step back and look at your motivations honestly. Does this seem like a once-in-a-lifetime chance to make millions? Is the possibility of a "quick score" driving your decision-making?

2. ***Be careful about trying to duplicate past successes.*** One of the worst things that can happen to a greedy investor is to have a highly successful investment: Your brother-in-law's second cousin's tip turns out to be right on the money, and you triple your initial investment in two months. As a greedy investor, you are absolutely convinced that you can make history repeat itself. Perhaps you act on another tip from this cousin. Perhaps you invest the same amount in a similar type of stock and expect to triple your money in two months. You may also have followed a system you read about in a book and when the system actually worked, you believe you have outsmarted the market and keep trying to make the system work again.

Whatever it is that worked, don't automatically assume it will work again. In fact, it probably won't. Things change so quickly that the conditions that helped a given investment work in June probably won't exist in July. Therefore, don't let your greed lock you into an unthinking investing pattern. Before using it again, use hindsight to get a clear view of why your initial investment paid off so handsomely. Did you happen to get lucky and put your money in a stock right before rumors of an acquisition circulated? Did your system of investing only in utility stocks work because an unusually hot summer nationwide created huge demands for electricity? Then ask yourself how likely it is that these conditions will repeat themselves.

3. ***Train yourself to spot "fool's gold" investments.*** Greedy investors are drawn to stocks that look like pure gold. Typically, the companies are selling products or services for which there seems to be a great need, and

these companies have a lock on the market. As their stock price shoots up, they seem too good to be true. Most of the time, they are. Some companies are in the right place at the right time, and they have their fifteen minutes of fame. If you're greedy, though, you may convince yourself that those fifteen minutes will last fifteen years. Taser International, the maker of stun guns, is an example of this type of company. When they announced a new contract to sell $1 million worth of stun guns to a local police department, the stock's market value rose $50 million in one day. In late 2004, the company's market value rose to over $2 billion, and they ended up making $19 million on revenue of $67 million for the year. While the stock did rise 360 percent in 2004, by 2006, Taser had given up most of that gain and dropped 80 percent. Many greedy investors bought Taser without considering that the valuations could never support the stock over time. They were blinded by Taser's spectacular take-off and could not see that it would soon come down to earth.

To avoid being similarly blinded, employ a certain amount of healthy skepticism when you encounter a skyrocketing stock. Force yourself to count to ten (figuratively speaking) and use that waiting time to do your homework. Remind yourself that most of the time, these incredibly, money-making stocks are not what they seem.

4. ***Satisfy your greed through a 5 percent limit.*** Limit the amount of money you put in "speculative" stocks and funds to 5 percent of your total investments. This limit will minimize the damage you do to your portfolio and perhaps satisfy the greed demons that drive you. Make sure, though, that this 5 percent limit isn't just in your mind. Greed has a funny way of ruining good intentions. Therefore, segregate this 5 percent fund into a separate brokerage account, preventing yourself from dipping into this account when a "can't miss" investment comes along and you want to invest more than you should.

In addition, do not use margin in this 5 percent account. As you are probably aware, margin is a line of credit within a brokerage account that allows you to purchase 50 percent more stock than the funds you have in the account. If you receive a margin call requiring you to put up more funds to cover losses, you may be tempted to take money from other sources, thereby violating your 5 percent limit.

5. ***Remind yourself daily that the market punishes the greedy and rewards the patient, long-term investor.*** Let us say that in 2000, you decided that you could make a bundle in the tech sector. One fund, Red Oak Select Technologies (ROGSX), appealed to you because they had recorded an amazing return of 126 percent in the previous year. You invested $10,000 in 2000, fully expecting to earn over 20 percent that first year and more than double your investment within a few years. Red Oak, however, returned minus 28.9 percent annually from 2000 to 2005. Your $10,000 investment would be down to $1,800.

Greedy investors are attracted to high-risk, high-reward investments, and more often than not, they receive the risk without the reward. Remind yourself of this fact. Despite all the stories you may have heard or read about people becoming phenomenally wealthy through their high-risk investing strategies, the individuals are anomalies. At best, they are playing a zero-sum game in which they win a lot and then lose a lot.

Remind yourself too, of these numbers: Long-term equity returns are around 11 percent and the very best equity managers can return 16 percent consistently. This is the top 1 percent over the long-term. While there are a few investors such as Warren Buffett who have returned far more, they make up just one in a thousand money managers. Over the short-term, returns can be much lower. If you find yourself investing with expectations that exceed these numbers, stop! Your desire for that 30 percent return will skew your investing strategy and in most cases cause you to lose money.

Identify the Greed-Based Decision-Making Points

The following scenario will give you an opportunity to identify the points where greed creates bad investment decision-making. Read through the scenario and see if you can find all the points at which greed skews this investor's judgment and causes him to make a flawed choice (The answers follow the scenario):

"John could not believe his luck. A vice president of a public relations agency, John had been interviewing candidates for an opening in his group, and the last candidate of the day was a young man, Mark, who was employed in an entry-level communications position at Gradalent Pharmaceutical. During the interview, Mark mentioned that among his responsibilities was writing news releases about promising studies Gradalent was conducting. One of those studies revolved around a weight loss medication that Mark confided was exceeding everyone's expectations. They had just received FDA approval for the product, but they were low-keying the announcement because they wanted to wait three months until the product was on the market and they could do a big PR push. According to Mark, Gradalent was going to spend a record amount of money marketing the weight loss product—they had budgeted more for advertising, public relations, and other promotional efforts than any weight loss product in history.

Within minutes after Mark left the office, John called his broker and instructed him to buy 2,000 shares of Gradalent at a share price of $25. John was not wealthy and he knew his wife would have a fit, but he figured this was his one chance to make a killing on the market, and that if he didn't act now, he would blow it. This was just the type of thing that happened to other people he knew—his brother-in-law had reaped a similar windfall when he invested in Apple right before they came out with the iPod—and he dreamed of similar riches. John also knew that Gradalent was one of the country's larger pharmaceutical companies and enjoyed a good reputation with a number of well-known products. Still, he had looked up the company on the Internet before calling his broker, and he had read an article written in one of the top business publications from a year ago praising the company's CEO and his strategy.

Within the month, the stock price had increased to $33 on increased publicity about the weight loss product. Positive news stories about the weight loss product were driving the price higher.

John called his broker again, ordering him to sell two other stocks he owned so he could invest an additional $10,000 in Gradalent. John figured that within a few months, product sales would be through the roof and $33 would be considered a bargain basement price.

The first cloud on the horizon came when a small story in the local newspaper reported that three women who were taking the Gradalent drug had been hospitalized with irregular heart rhythms. A spokesman for Gradalent said that not a single person in their extensive studies had reported arrhythmias caused by the drug, and the article quoted a medical doctor as saying that since all three women taking the weight loss drug were at least forty-five years of age and overweight, it was unlikely that the drug was the culprit. Nonetheless, the stock price went down to $27 on the news.

John saw this as a great opportunity to make even more money, and he immediately called his broker and bought $10,000 more of Gradalent.

The following week, a story broke in a leading business journal reporting that Gradalent was under investigation by a government agency for covering up negative results in the testing of their weight loss drug; that a number of people in the study had experienced heart problems, including irregular heart rhythms. The stock price went down to $19.

John talked to his broker about the troubles Gradalent was experiencing, but he rejected his recommendation that he sell even one share of stock. John refused to believe that the cover-up would be anything more than a temporary setback. After all, no one had died from the heart problems. The article noted that it was possible Gradalent was not responsible for at least some of these medical problems, since the participants themselves didn't connect their symptoms to the weight loss drug and never filled out an official form reporting any significant medical problems.

Two weeks later, when Gradalent had gone down to $12, all hell broke loose. A bigger investigative piece broke in the local business journal, revealing that Gradalent's CEO was about to be indicted for orchestrating a cover-up of negative results not just for the weight loss drug but for other products as well; that this CEO had a history of playing fast and loose with the rules in previous corporate positions; and that the company had an unusually large amount of debt, a fact that had been reported in a number of articles over the past six months.

Gradalent filed for bankruptcy less than a year later.”

The following are the bad choices John made that were caused by his greed:

Bad Choice #1: John invested too much too fast based on skimpy information. He was so anxious to capitalize on "inside information" and make his fortune that he didn't learn much about Gradalent. While price information may not have been illegal to act on, at a minimum it certainly raised ethical questions.

Bad Choice #2: John bought more stock at a price that was $8 more than he originally paid, and he made his portfolio less diversified in the process. He was so myopically greedy for maximum profit that he did not recognize he was committing a double sin—not only was he being greedy, but he was lusting after a stock that was not worthy of him.

Bad Choice #3: When the first report of problems with Gradalent's study broke and the stock went down to $27, John should have decreased his position in the stock. It is what any prudent investor would have done, since he still would have come close to breaking even. Greed, though, made it impossible for John to let go of his dream of striking it rich. In fact, it spurred him to buy more Gradalent, a completely illogical move.

Bad Choice #4: When the price went down to $19, he should have gotten rid of the stock. It was clearly about to enter free fall, but John's greed caused him to rationalize Gradalent's problems and cause him to be optimistic when there was no reason for optimism.

Demonstrate Discipline When Greed Strikes

Realistically, greed is such a powerful force at times that it's difficult to find that coolly rational place that allows you to stop your investing reflex. You come across a stock that you're convinced is going to take off, and you feel every second you delay represents many dollars lost. In these situations, it's all you can do not to sell the house and use the proceeds for this investment.

Developing a disciplined mindset can help you deal with these tempting situations. By disciplined, I mean you must be in a highly conscious, analytical state when you make an investment decision. Even as your greed is pushing you to rush forward or buy more, your discipline provides you with more rational alternatives. How do you develop discipline? I've suggested a few techniques earlier, such as imposing a 5 percent limit and gathering sufficient information before acting. Here are some additional ways to do so:

USE A METHOD OR A PROCESS BEFORE MAKING AN INVESTMENT DECISION

Whether it's going through a mental checklist of things you need to do before taking action or employing a series of questions that must be answered to your satisfaction, a process ensures that you won't act based only on an overwhelming desire to make money quickly.

GIVE YOURSELF FLEXIBILITY

In the grip of greed, investors often feel that they have only once choice: They must buy 1,000 shares of stock X immediately! A disciplined investor will logically analyze alternatives to this compelling action. Instead of buying 1,000 shares, perhaps he might buy 1,100. Instead of buying the shares now, he might wait and observe for a few days and see how things are shaking out. After the initial purchase emotion subsides. Often it is best to scale into an investment and give yourself flexibility to purchase at lower prices given the opportunity—it is best not to commit your maximum dollars at the initial entry point.

CREATE A WORST-CASE SCENARIO

In other words, have the discipline to play devil's advocate and look at what your greed is not telling you. If you sell your 5,000 shares in IBM and decide to invest all of it in a start-up, high-tech company, what are the odds that you might lose everything? How many high-tech start-ups have gone under in the past year? What percentage start with great promise and publicity and then turn in mediocre performances? What would happen if the hotshot CEO who is the company's heart and soul decided to leave or violates the law in some way; does he have a history of quitting on companies or of unethical behavior? You don't want to be overly pessimistic, but you do want the advantage of knowing what the negative results of your greed might be.

DO A LONG-TERM, RISK-REWARD CALCULATION

If you're a greedy investor, you've probably already done your short-term calculation. You've determined that the chances of making a lot of money right away greatly outweigh the risks. Whether true or not, this is often the way avarice shapes our thinking. Counter this with a long-term calculation: Is this investment likely to help achieve the goals I've set for myself twenty years hence without too much risk; is there another investment that will better help me meet these needs with a reasonable amount of risk?

Discipline is a useful tool to manage all seven sins, but it is particularly important for greed, since that sin often compels us to act quickly and without analysis or reflection.

Finally, if greed is your number one sin, be aware that you're suffering from an affliction that plagued people throughout history and especially when it came to financial decisions.

The Talmud, which is the basis of many Jewish laws, addressed the concept of greed over 1,000 years ago with the passage: "If you try to grab too much, you may end up with nothing."

In literature, the theater, and the movies, a character's downfall is often greed. It is a completely believable catalyst for the negative events that befall a character, since everyone is acutely aware of how powerful a force greed can be. Recognize, though, that you can decrease the power of greed over your investing if you recognize when it's affecting your decisions and you make a concerted effort to minimize its impact—by imposing discipline upon yourself.

6

Anger/Wrath

Don't Get Mad, Get Even (at the Very Least)

There is nothing like the fury of an investor scorned. While CEOs of companies, brokers, and newsletter gurus don't do this scorning directly, that's often what it feels like to people vulnerable to this sin. Investors frequently feel betrayed, cheated, and stupid, and these feelings generate tremendous amounts of anger. While everyone becomes angry at some point in his investing life, not everyone allows this anger to color his judgment and influence his decision-making; professional investors learn to wall off their anger and other strong emotions from their decision-making. Investing-related anger can be irrational, but it can also be completely justified. Investment advisors do make bad recommendations, and CEOs of companies make ill-conceived moves that drive the stock price down unexpectedly, and if you're caught holding a lot of the stock, you have every right to be furious.

The problem occurs when you invest in a state of high dudgeon. On the surface, anger is energizing. It feels good to do something about the anger rather than just sit and stew. As an angry investor, you are eager to get back in the game, to show the person who made you angry that you're not stupid or naïve. Many times, you're not even furious at one person but at the market in general, a seemingly odd reaction since the market is a vast and indifferent force. In reality, though, investors frequently personify the market: when it's doing well, they love it, when it turns on them, they hate it. Angry investors need to feel angry at someone, and if they lack a particular person to blame, they attribute human characteristics to the market: Fickle, sadistic, and manipulative are just some of the printable terms angry investors use.

For angry investors, resisting the impulse to invest when in the grip of this powerful emotion may seem unnatural. It is almost a reflex: You get hit, you hit back. But this is a counterproductive reflex, one that causes you to make decisions in the heat of the moment that can cost you a great deal later on. The sin of wrath is especially powerful—few emotions course through us with more force than anger—but there are ways to resist giving in to it. To help you resist, let's look at who investors get angry with and how this anger influences their decision-making.

Targets of Wrath

As we noted, angry investors sometimes lack a specific target and disperse their anger over the market in general. They rant about the market's cruelty and indifference, and it is like ranting about fate. Many times, though, investors focus their anger on a specific person, group, or event. In some instances, this target is worthy of their ire—a CEO made a bad decision that negatively affected the stock price. In other instances, however, investors made mistakes and set up targets as scapegoats—they blame others for their oversights and lack of due diligence. Understanding what the common targets are and how they trigger our anger gives us a weapon to defend ourselves against it. Keep the following targets in mind the next time you find yourself furious at them for an investing loss:

THE MEDIA

The media is a convenient target for all types of people in all types of situations. Athletes scream when they are misquoted and politicians rage against what they perceive as unfair coverage. Investors often assign blame to the media for spreading rumor, bias, and lies. They hate a particular columnist for letting everyone in on an investment they feel is their secret or they despise publications that create a selling panic in a sector in which they are heavily invested. The problem here is that investors react as if the media is an adversary, and they want to beat them at their own game. George, for instance, became outraged when CNBC, the *Wall St. Journal,* and other media outlets began revealing negative information about earning revisions at Enron. His 1,000-share position, which he acquired at $30 per share, began to drop. At the time (2001), George believed that Enron was a good company that may have made a few mistakes, but that it was being singled out by the media for punishment. It appeared to George that the media had it in for Enron precisely because they were a highly successful company, and that they were going after the biggest and the best. He was extremely upset, and he reacted by buying an additional 4,000 shares. This nose-thumbing gesture was expensive, but it made George feel good. At least it made him feel good until more unethical practices emerged and the share price hit $8 and kept on dropping. Eventually, George's anger at the media was replaced by his anger at Ken Lay and Jeffrey Skilling.

CEOS

Heads of companies are highly visible targets. I have seen investors exhibit tremendous hostility toward a corporation's CEO, convinced that a few bad decisions ruined the company or set the stock price plummeting. Even when this is an accurate accusation, the anger overwhelms judgment. In some instances, it causes furious investors to sell their stock in a good company prematurely because they can't stand the CEO. While the CEO may have made a bad decision, it may not mean he is incompetent. Even if he is incompetent, the organization may still be productive and profitable. To allow your animosity toward one person in a company of thousands dictate your investing strategy isn't a good idea. As important as CEOs are, other factors must be analyzed before deciding to sell all your holdings. Anger at a CEO can also cause investors to try and "get back at them" by selling their holdings and investing in a competitor. Again, this may be a wise move, but it requires more than a revenge motive as its basis.

AN INVESTMENT ADVISOR/FINANCIAL ANALYST

At one point or another, investment advisors offer bad advice and financial analysts issue bad buy, hold, or sell recommendations. This is the nature of the business, and the best advisors and analysts have a good batting average in the long term. Nonetheless, people who are vulnerable to this sin can erupt when advice doesn't pan out. They become so angry that not only do they fire the advisor but they pursue an investing strategy that is diametrically opposed to the one their advisor (or an analyst) advocated. If their advisor was conservative, they start taking a lot of risks. If their advisor suggested that Fund X was poorly managed and they should avoid it, they immediately put money into it. They are so angry that they invest through "opposing reaction." This is obviously a terrible way to invest, but when people see red, they also convince themselves they see black. They want to prove to the advisor that they were right all along and that they were fools to listen to anything he said. Unconsciously, they assume that because their advisor recommended the wrong thing, doing the right thing will produce a profit. Anger skews our logic and results in ridiculous syllogisms such as this one.

A GROUP WITH A VESTED INTEREST

You may be furious with the Feds for a change in interest rates or with the FDA for turning down a pharmaceutical company's request for approval of a new drug after your investment was predicated on that approval. You might also become angry with a union for striking a company or with a major civil rights group for filing a discrimination lawsuit against an organization in which you hold stock. This anger causes you to scream, "I'm never going to invest in a pharmaceutical company again," or "I'm putting my money into a stock where the company has never had a whiff of scandal." You are so angry at a given group that you create an investing strategy based on your dislike of a group's actions. It may satisfy your initial need never to make the same mistake twice and your anger at making it the first time, but it is completely irrational.

By identifying these four targets of anger, you can watch for instances when you are tempted to make an investing decision with one of these targets in mind. Reading this now, you may think that you'll never invest in anger. In truth, many of us do and rationalize what we did after the fact. We don't admit to ourselves that we made an investment because we wanted to show a hated columnist that we know more than he does or that we sold all our shares in a blue-chip company because we couldn't stand the CEO. Therefore, ask yourself the following question before you make an investment decision:

"Who am I angry at now?"

To give you a better sense of how anger can get the best of even smart and savvy investors, let me tell you about Nathan, a successful film producer who handles all his own investing. For a number of years, Nathan had been a shareholder in Elan Corporation, PLC (ELN), an Irish pharmaceutical company focusing on advanced therapies relating to autoimmune diseases. By February 25, 2005, Nathan owned 5,000 shares of Elan, which closed at a price of $27 per share. Like any drug company, Elan lived and died by the products it developed. Unlike Pfizer, Eli Lilly, and other huge pharmaceutical companies, though, Elan was not nearly as diversified. As a result, when a patient died after taking their multiple sclerosis drug, Elan suspended sales on February 28, 2005, the stock price was hit hard. Elan fell 19 points to 8, a loss of 70 percent. This one drug was projected to bring in revenue of $4 billion by 2009, and now there was talk of withdrawing it.

Nathan raged against what he believed to be an overreaction to one death. He was upset at the market for turning its back on a terrific company; he was furious at the FDA for their saber-rattling warnings; he was seething whenever he read or heard a story that suggested doom and gloom for Elan; and he was mad at the company for not defending itself more vigorously. When bonds matured in his brokerage account around this time, Nathan took the money and invested it in 10,000 more shares of Elan at $8 a share.

When reading about this decision now, it seems hopelessly irrational. Who would invest more money in a company with these serious problems? An angry investor would. To Nathan, his wrath had overcome all rational objections to the investment. In a strange way, his investment was a statement of principle: He believed in Elan, he was convinced they had been unfairly tarred and he was going to put his money where his mouth was. At the time, his anger clouded his thinking and convinced him that in time, the wrong done to Elan would be righted and he would benefit. Nathan felt his anger was righteous, and that investing more money in the company was justified by the righteousness of his position.

Of course, when the drug was withdrawn from the market, analysts lowered their price target and the stock fell to $5, Nathan's anger began to ebb and he began to reflect on his investing behaviors. Only with hindsight did he see how his anger led him to make a poor investment, and it was only then that he began to sell off his stock in Elan.

Differentiating Between Normal and Sinful Anger

Because anger is such a common investing emotion, how do you know if it's impacting your decision-making? Start out by considering the following list of sinfully angry investor versus normally angry investor traits:

Sinfully Angry

— Never blames himself for an investment that goes bad

— Always seeks scapegoats upon which he can vent his frustration for losses

— Makes investing decisions in the heat of the moment

— Finds the market more aggravating and stressful than just about anything else in his life

— Is only able to relieve angry feelings by making another investment

— Falls into a pattern whereby major investment decisions are immediately preceded by losing temper

— Views investing as a macho competition where aggressive, instinctive behavior is rewarded

Normally Angry

— Is often upset with himself when he suffers an investment loss

— Usually avoids blaming others or making excuses when an investment doesn't work out

— Allows anger to dissipate before making an investment decision

— Becomes upset with investments and related news about the market but no more so than in other areas of life

— Making an investment has no impact on feelings of anger

— Has no discernible pattern when it comes to anger and making an investment

— Sees investing as a cerebral activity that rewards analysis and objectivity and tries to avoid strong emotions such as anger in the decision-making process

The last trait on the Sinfully Angry list should be of special concern, since it seems to be increasingly prevalent among investors (especially men) who view this as an intensely competitive activity. If you have ever met a professional trader—someone who works at the Chicago Mercantile Exchange, for instance—you've probably met this type. They invest with a chip on their shoulders and a snarl in their voices (the Merc is "open outcry" trading). They approach trading as combat—you're either a winner or a loser—and they often possess a belligerent, hostile attitude. They believe the winners are the fiercest warriors, and so they trade with great aggression.

This is absolutely the wrong posture for investors with long-term goals. During my years at Salomon Brothers, I encountered a few of these trading personalities, who played what they termed a "zero-sum" game. Loud and harsh, these individuals may have done well in the short-term at times, but usually they shot themselves in the foot in the long run. Their tendency to blame others for their mistakes rather than learn from what they did wrong caused them to repeat these mistakes. On the other hand, the best traders at Salomon Brothers were the most level-headed of the bunch. Professional and polite, they fenced off their anger. Not only did they prevent it from influencing their decision-making, but it was rare to see them yelling or angry at any point during the day. It's not surprising that many from this level-headed group went on to start hedge funds and other lucrative trading platforms that earned them many millions of dollars.

Therefore, be wary of adopting an angry, battling persona as your investing personality. It shouldn't be surprising that women are often much better able to resist this temptation than men, who view investing as a form of gamesmanship and see this activity as a way to prove their worth. In long-term investing, patient, calm, objective people are rewarded and hot-headed ones are punished.

Anger Management: How to Stop Your Rage from Getting the Best of You

Anger becomes a deadly investing sin when it isn't managed. Anger in itself isn't a problem; the actions it prompts you to take, though, can cause major losses. To help you prevent these losses, here are two sets of tips. The first relates to monitoring your investing moods; the second involves avoiding specific, anger-induced investing mistakes.

Mood Monitor

If you're vulnerable to the sin of wrath, you need to be vigilant for signs of anger in all its forms when you're contemplating your investments. Be alert for the following emotions and take the suggested precautions if you spot them:

1. ***A red-hot desire for vengeance.*** You want revenge against the market in general or a broker who you feel gave you bad advice or the media for ruining a great investment. When you're contemplating a given investment, all you can think about is how the "enemy" will rue the day they crossed you. Your goal is not financial as much as it is that sweet feeling of defeating your adversary.

If this sounds like you, you need to give yourself a ten count. Specifically, wait ten days before making any investment decisions. No matter whether someone has really done you wrong and vengeance is justified, you need to step away from what's pushing you powerfully toward a decision that may not be in your best interest. Time usually takes the edge off the desire for vengeance. This ten-day cooling down period is especially useful when vengeance is the predominant feeling, since the desire to exact it is usually immediate and commanding.

2. ***Fury at yourself or others for making "stupid" mistakes.*** You can't believe you invested in a stock right before it plunged and you beat yourself up for your lack of foresight. You are apoplectic because you have a large position in a utility fund and the fund manager just resigned amid scandal; you knew about the manager's checkered past and yet you rationalized it. You are steaming mad at your advisor because he misinterpreted your instructions and bought the wrong stock, which had performed poorly.

You're furious at yourself or others for doing something stupid, and your impulse is to act immediately to get rid of that feeling of being stupid. You are so angry at yourself, you want to do something now rather than take a little while to assess what went wrong and what the best next step is.

The key here is analysis. To diminish that feeling of being dumb, try and understand what caused you to be victimized by a stupid mistake. Ask yourself if it was caused by:

- A failure to do your homework about an investment or source of advice
- Bad luck

- Being stressed out and lacking the time to make a thoughtful decision

- Moving too quickly

Analysis is a good antidote to all the seven sins, but it is especially useful when anger is involved. Knowledge about why you made an investing error doesn't ameliorate its effect, but it does give you some perspective that can stop you from acting in anger. Therefore, analyze the stupidity. Create a written analysis of what went wrong and why. Detail what you might have done to prevent the idiotic mistake.

3. ***Anger at the poor performance of an investment.*** While you may also be peeved at a specific individual who you believe is responsible for a loss, your anger centers on the specific stock, bond, or fund that has "let you down." So much of our ego is tied up in our investing that when an investment's performance doesn't meet our expectations, we are hurt. It calls into question our abilities and our perceptions, and rather than accepting that we were the victims of fate (a scary thought!) or that we simply made a mistake, we become defensive and angry. In this state, we become dangerous to our portfolios. We want to get rid of the offending investment and find a new and better one. We're so angry at how the investment performance thwarted our expectations that we want to do something about it.

In most instances, though, watchful waiting is a better response. Too often, angry investors are volatile investors, switching investments as soon as one disappoints and infuriates them. While there are times when investments are worth jettisoning, angry investors usually need to curb their impulse to kick an offending investment out of the portfolio.

If this is your impulse, buy yourself a bit of time by examining your rationale for the investment initially. Ask yourself:

— What was your reasoning for making the investment?

— Were you acting on an inside tip, on accumulated information from different sources, on instinct?

— Despite whatever negative events caused your investment not to live up to your expectations, is your original investing rationale still valid?

— If you were coming to this investment fresh—if you were considering it for the first time—would it be attractive to you?

— Are there any completely separate investments from this one where you might direct your energies; is there another area where you can calmly and rationally make an investment?

These questions will help you calm down and reassess the investment as well as find another, more appropriate way to use your investing energy. Often, the best strategy for angry investors is to calm down, reassess, hold on, and consider unrelated opportunities. The following story illustrates this.

In the summer of 1999, I saw the "froth" on the NASDAQ market and found the valuations outrageous. The prices of Internet stocks such as Yahoo, eBay, Cisco, and WebMD were the sprinkles on the froth. I began to short this sector by selling naked calls on the street.com index. In other words, I would profit if the Internet stocks fell and lose money if they rose. From July 1999 to December 1999, the index rose by over 100 percent.

Anger is not the sin to which I'm particularly vulnerable, but during this period, I was furious. Most of the time, I was angry with myself for thinking I could outsmart the market. By March, the index had risen another 15 percent from the beginning of the year, and I remember seeing a CNBC report that hyped the market and being outraged that they were perpetuating a myth. Similarly, I was angry at my colleagues who had been swept up in Internet fever and were making money while I was losing it. And most of all, I was angry at my brilliant strategy because it was failing so miserably.

I could have bailed out at that point—I remember the painful confession to my wife that we had lost 20 percent of our net worth on this strategy—but I did what I recommend you do: reviewed my investing rationale and determined its current viability. Despite my losses, it seemed more viable than ever. So I hung in there, and I also continued to assess other opportunities. After doing a considerable amount of research, I discovered that certain non-tech stocks were significantly undervalued. I decided to add to my short position and used the proceeds to buy a basket of depressed value stocks including Exelon Corporation, Countrywide Financial, and North Fork Bank.

In the next few months, everything turned around. The street.com index plummeted 75 percent by the end of the year. In addition, my base of undervalued stocks soared, increasing my portfolio's value by over 50 percent that year. Looking back, I know I didn't follow my own advice—I should never have let my pride and my anger put my net worth in such serious jeopardy. Fortunately, I also managed that anger after a while and ended up coming out ahead.

Certain types of investing seem to trigger anger in certain investors, and if you're vulnerable to this sin, you should do everything possible to avoid these types. Specifically, *don't:*

1. SEEK HIGHLY VOLATILE, MICROCAP STOCK INVESTMENTS

These stocks are thinly traded and not widely followed, and they can spike up or down 25 percent on hints and rumors. In addition these speculative securities are frequently sold to institutional investors and insiders at prices far below the market, and when they in turn sell, prices can drop precipitously. Few things spark more anger in investors than sudden, precipitous drops in price. If you're prone to angry investing, you'll react to these drops by doubling down or looking for a better microcap, and you'll probably get burned again. If you must invest in this sector, do so through a mutual fund. Otherwise, you're just asking for trouble because these notoriously volatile stocks are infuriating even to the pros.

2. BUY A STOCK JUST TO CATCH THE MOMENTUM TRADE

People who commit the sin of wrath should steer clear of investments that inexplicably plummet. Technical trades can look good numerically but perform badly for no discernible reason. Out of the blue, a stock that has good technicals and is on the rise can suddenly reverse direction. This can set off your anger response, since you often can search in vain for an explanation of why it took a nosedive. Anger feeds on uncertainty, so avoid technical trades since they are often purely a numbers game.

3. INVEST BLINDLY BASED ONLY A FRIEND'S OR A COLLEAGUE'S RECOMMENDATIONS OR SOME OTHER TYPE OF RUMOR OR INSIDE TIP

More often than not, angry investors blame the messenger. Their investing anger reflex kicks in when they make an investment based primarily on what someone told them and it doesn't work out. With hindsight, they realize that they were given bad advice and that they were fools to take it in the first place. As a result, they become incredibly angry and put themselves in a dangerous investing frame of mind. Angry investors need to be especially focused on doing their homework, on analyzing carefully, and on adopting a conservative strategy.

4. TRADE ON THE DAY THAT NEWS COMES OUT

If a piece of news makes you angry—the CEO is indicted, an analyst downgrades a company, economic data suggests a downturn affecting a particular industry—give yourself time to digest the news. Wait at least a day before making an investment. Typically, angry investors sell too quickly or buy more stock at the wrong price because they are overreacting to fresh news. If you give yourself at least twenty-four hours before making a decision, you'll probably calm down enough not to make a mistake . . . or to make less of a mistake than you ordinarily would.

Take the Emotion out of Investing: How to Stay Cool When the Process Can Be So Infuriating

For all the seven sins, the goal is to keep your emotions in check when making investment decisions, but it is especially important here. Anger flares up faster than any of the other sins and it can be so powerful that before you know it, you've made an ill-advised investment. Besides the previous recommendations, here are some proactive steps that can keep your anger out of the process:

FORCE YOURSELF TO TAKE BREAKS FROM THE INVESTMENT WORLD IN GENERAL AND YOUR PORTFOLIO IN PARTICULAR

The more you immerse yourself in an investing mindset, the angrier you're likely to get, especially if things aren't going your way. Rubbing your nose in your own mistakes or the market's unpleasant surprises for hours every day will just raise your hackles. As a long-term investor, you don't need to be tracking your stocks nonstop or be up on every market development. While I strongly advocate being aware of events that have an impact on your portfolio, you can maintain this awareness by monitoring it every few days or by spending just a little time on it daily. Reducing your exposure to the investing world will reduce your aggravation. You will be less likely to blow your stack or your investment dollars from the accumulated pain associated with nonstop market monitoring.

REMIND YOURSELF THAT IT'S BUSINESS, NOT PERSONAL

It's sometimes difficult to remember that the market isn't out to get you, since it sometimes seems to wait for you to make an investment move and then heads in the opposite direction. In reality, the market is as coolly indifferent to the charitable grandmother from Topeka as it is to the shark-like professional trader. You may recognize this fact intellectually, but part of you wants to imbue the market with human traits, especially negative ones. Just as primitive man blamed the gods for drought and blight, we blame the market for our losses. Reflexively, we shake our first at both the heavens and the market gods.

For investors susceptible to the sin of anger, this reflex is dangerous. When we are convinced the market has it in for us, we become paranoid and enraged. We lose our objectivity and end up fighting the market rather than going with it.

Remind yourself periodically that you should not take your investing losses personally. Try and adopt a more Zen-like perspective and accept both the good and bad things that happen to you as an investor as equal and related forces. Let your mantra be, "Investing is business, not personal."

KEEP AN INVESTING/ANGER JOURNAL

Sometimes people change their behaviors only when they have direct evidence that these behaviors are counterproductive. Keeping a journal that charts your investing decisions over a short period of time (a month or two) and the mood you were in when you made these decisions can provide irrefutable evidence that anger leads to losses. It is proactive in the sense that it may help you spot a trend before it results in major losses. In the journal, note the date and time of all investments and whether you were particularly angry at someone or something when you made the investment decision. Specify whom you were angry at and how that anger catalyzed a given investment. Put the journal aside after a month or two and revisit each investment later in the year, noting which investments were bad ones. See if there is a correspondence between anger and losses (or mediocre performance).

Another benefit to this journal is that it makes you more aware of when you buy or sell in the heat of the moment. The act of writing draws your attention to your emotional state at the time of an investing decision. When you write, "I decided to sell my shares in X because I was furious with my broker who recommended it, and it's done nothing but go down. I can't wait to rub it in his face when it trades lower, since he seems so certain that it won't," you capture your feelings in a way that you can't ignore. Over time, you may identify a pattern of anger that will serve as a red flag whenever you invest.

If you have a good memory and are anxious to benefit from this journal immediately, take out your brokerage statements from six months ago and try and remember which investments you made in anger and which ones delivered disappointing results. With hindsight, you may see the connection between anger and poor investing.

VENT YOUR ANGER PRODUCTIVELY

This last point may be the most important of all the suggestions in this section. I am not a psychologist, but I do know that there are productive and unproductive ways to deal with this powerful emotion. Just as you shouldn't invest when you're in a rage, neither should you try and swallow that rage and pretend it doesn't exist. When you're furious with the market or your broker or you think the CEO of a company in which you have stock made a boneheaded decision, you need to do something about it (besides making an investment decision). Some people need to blow off steam by playing racquetball or some other sport. Others need to write a letter to the editor or e-mail the head of a fund about what they feel was a stupid move. When I was watching my portfolio dwindle and waiting for the overvalued Internet stocks to fall, I found that when I talked to my wife or a colleague about the situation, it helped diminish my anger and prevented it from surfacing while I was making investment choices. Expressing your anger to a sympathetic listener can be a great way to vent without disturbing your portfolio.

If you are using a broker or advisor, you might want to call him or make a date for lunch to talk about what has you upset. Good brokers/advisors are like doctors; they have heard it all before and can allay irrational fears, explain the positive ramifications of seemingly negative events and generally put anger-causing people and problems into perspective. Of course, if your broker/advisor is the cause of your anger, you may want to give yourself a cooling-off period before talking to him.

Finally, the Internet provides numerous forums and message boards where you can express your disappointment and dissatisfaction with a given stock, bond, fund, broker, CEO, or other offending party. While you have to be careful about taking the information on various sites as gospel—sometimes people have axes to grind or rumors to spread—they are great for getting the anger out of your system. I have found the Yahoo stock message board at http://finance.yahoo.com to be especially useful for venting. All you need to do when you get on the site is type on the ticker of the stock and you will be directed to the summary page for the selected stock. Along the left side you will find a link, "message board." Not only can you read messages from people who may be angry about the same issues that you are—misery loves company—but you can distill your wrath into a few well-chosen sentences and ask questions.

7

Gluttony

How Not to Consume the Market Before It Consumes You

Gluttons are addicts, only instead of being hooked on food they crave the action of trading. While people who eat a lot may grow large, people who invest a lot often see their portfolios shrink. This type of investor sells bad stocks in the hope of finding good ones and sells good performers in the hope of finding better ones. Even if they have an outstanding investment, they tend to convince themselves that it has peaked and that they would be wise to sell it sooner rather than later. They also buy anything and everything. Not to belabor our analogy, but like a fat person approaching a buffet, they want to try some of everything. They are just as likely to buy a blue chip stock as make a wildly speculative investment.

They operate on the assumption that more is better; that the more stocks, bonds, and funds they buy and sell, the better their results. They are never satisfied with their portfolio and always feel compelled to change it in some way. The action of investing is the only thing that satisfies them, but it only satisfies them for a brief period of time.

Gluttony makes it virtually impossible to have a successful, long-term strategy. Constant buying and selling not only results in high transaction costs and taxes, but makes it more difficult to be objective, reflective, and analytical. In short, it argues against adopting the approach that is the hallmark of the best investors.

Are you guilty of gluttony? Before deciding if this sin applies to you, consider some specific traits of investing gluttony.

Signs of an Investor Whose Eyes Are Bigger Than His Stomach

It's likely that most investors, at some point in their investing careers, buy and sell much too quickly. Perhaps they get caught up in a market upturn or downswing or they are going through a difficult period in their personal lives and turn to day trading as a form of escape. If overactive trading is an anomaly rather than a pattern, then you probably aren't guilty of this sin. On the other hand, if you find that you periodically fall into the habit of overactive investing, gluttony may be a problem you need to address.

I recognize that gluttony can be a tricky sin to identify, since "overactive" is a subjective term. Therefore, let's look at the specific traits of investing gluttons:

BUYING IN THE WORST POSSIBLE MARKETS

Most people steer clear of investing when the markets plunge. While opportunities exist to cherry-pick in a down market, investors should be highly selective and analytical when it seems as if everything is going south. Investing gluttons, though, convince themselves that they can find the few winners amid the overwhelming number of losers. On a day when the broad market averages are all negative, gluttons recognize that a handful of stocks will still rise 10 percent or more. Their problem is that they buy indiscriminately, lacking the patience for a true good buy to emerge. Invariably, they are lured in by stocks and funds that glitter on the surface but have little of substance to justify a buy.

Gluttons are famous for taking one piece of positive information and going to town on it. They use one piece of good news amid the bad to justify their investment.

VIEWING THEIR INVESTING WITH FALSE OPTIMISM

Gluttons invest with a smile on their face and hope in their heart. In their minds, they rationalize losses and exaggerate wins, making it seem as if they are far better investors than they really are. They tell people that their investments are doing great, even when they haven't even been doing well. In many instances, this optimism is a result of ignorance. They really haven't been following their investments closely, and they selectively tell themselves the good news and ignore the bad.

BECOMING A 24/7 INVESTOR

In other words, investing spills over into other aspects of their lives. Not only do they get up from the dinner table to call their broker but they make excuses about why they can't go on family outings in order to attend an investing seminar. More than that, they are constantly thinking about investing techniques and tactics and have a distracted air about them. They may also neglect their jobs, getting in trouble at work or being fired because they are so focused on making the next investment.

INVESTING HEAVILY IN SMALL CAP STOCKS AND OPTIONS

Because of their volatility and their potential for profit, these stocks appeal to gluttons. Small caps generally represent a company with a total stock market value of under $500 million. People invest in small caps dreaming about picking the next Yahoo, Dell, or Microsoft, but they usually end up picking a stock that goes nowhere—or that goes bust. Later, I'll suggest a way that gluttons can use to invest in small caps without the compulsive behavior that often dooms their investment. This is a sector noted for insider selling and private equity placements at prices well below the market. If you enter small caps grabbing stocks left and right and relying mostly on your instincts rather than on any real knowledge, you're likely to make big mistakes.

The price action of options, too, appeals to the glutton. If you're not a professional investor, you probably are not in a good position to evaluate option pricing on a real-time basis or know whether it makes sense to buy or sell a call or put. Nonetheless, trading options has the feel of "hardcore" investing, and it provides a thrill for someone who can't get enough of it.

DAY TRADING

Day trading can be associated with a variety of sins, but it is especially common with gluttony. It feeds the glutton's habit of making a lot of trades quickly. Of course, it also offers the chance to rack up a lot of commissions and other transaction costs.

BUYING HOT STOCKS AFTER THEY'VE REACHED THEIR PEAK

Gluttons often go after stocks that everyone and their brothers know are hot. Licking their chops, they buy stocks after a strong earnings report has been issued or after they announced the introduction of a breakthrough drug (or some similarly impressive piece of news). Gluttons assume that the superior performance will continue, even though it's much more likely that the stock has reached or is close to its high point. Nonetheless, gluttons are so hungry to be part of a successful investment that they tell themselves the upward trend they've observed will continue indefinitely.

Maria embodies a number of these traits. A well-compensated 35-year-old business executive, Maria spends an inordinate amount of her free time on her investments. In fact, she often closes her door at work and calls her broker when an investment idea occurs to her. Though she has resisted day trading, Maria relishes options, small caps, and other investing approaches that require considerable time and effort. Maria considers herself a "real" investor, unlike friends and colleagues who she privately scoffs at as "dabblers." She believes you can't get good at something unless you enmesh yourself in it, and Maria is seriously enmeshed. She hates sitting on any investment for a significant period of time, convinced that she'll never make as much money sitting on the sidelines while others are buying and selling and improving their position. Maria's life is basically her work and her investing. On more than one occasion, her relationships with men have suffered, as she has been so focused on her work and investing she doesn't have time right now in her life for marriage or children. Though she likes the idea of some day settling down and having a family, right now she can't imagine sacrificing her investing time. Maria rationalizes that if she keeps investing at her current pace, she's bound to strike it rich, and then perhaps she will consider cutting back.

In 2000, Maria's division exceeded their performance targets by a considerable margin, and she received a $200,000 bonus. She divided the investment among four stocks: Redback, Terayon, Allstate, and Wachovia Bank. Maria expected a great deal of upward action from these stocks, but they remained relatively static for the next four weeks. At the end of that period, Maria had had enough. She felt she might as well place her bonus in her checking account. Fortunately, Redback started to make some noise, and Maria had a hunch that the computer networking company was going to take off. She transferred the entire $200,000 into Redback, and it lost 25 percent in three weeks. Undeterred, Maria moved the remaining bonus money into Terayon, a cable box company that had gone dormant after appreciating 250 percent in the nine months prior to her purchase. Maria figured that the dormant period was just about over and it was ready to go on another upward surge. Instead, it went on a downward spiral and Maria was left with $30,000 of her original bonus. Interestingly, Allstate and Wachovia moved slowly but steadily upward during this period, and if Maria would simply have stuck with her original investment in all four companies, she would have come out ahead.

Four Weaknesses: Why Gluttons Invariably Lose Money

Like Maria, most gluttons rationalize their investing behaviors. They equate action with money: You've got to play if you want it to pay. This may be true if you are a trader in Chicago Board of Trade, but for the rest of us, frenetic investing usually results in losses rather than in wins. Gluttons invest burdened by four weaknesses that they may be unaware of or that they may discount. Let's examine these four vulnerabilities and why they should not be discounted:

COMMISSIONS

The more trades you make, the more commissions you pay. If you're paying $8 a trade, you can do many trades before this fee makes a dent in your return. Many gluttons, however, like using brokers—it makes them feel more a part of the professional action—and some brokers charge $50 or more per transaction. This can cut into their returns, adding between three and ten cents per trade. Typically, these investors justify these commissions, telling themselves that by being active traders, they ultimately make enough money to compensate themselves for commissions paid. In most instances, of course, this is not true.

BID-ASK DIFFERENTIAL

This is the difference between where the market is willing to buy the stock (bid) and where the best offer to sell (ask) is. With a liquid stock like Microsoft, the differential may be as little as 2 cents on a $25 price or about .08 percent. Because gluttons often trade in more volatile, speculative stocks, they must endure wider bid-ask differentials. For example, a stock like Royal Financial (RYFL.OB) on a given day had a bid-ask difference of one-quarter point on a $13 share price. This is about 2 percent of the value of the stock, adding a significant amount to the trading cost.

SHORT-TERM GAINS

Higher income investors are taxed at a rate of 35 percent on these gains. For investments held longer than one year, the rate drops to 15 percent. People who buy and sell at a rapid clip, therefore, are penalized because they are simply unable to hold onto the investment for more than a year. Not only must investors pay short-term gains on investments in the year they are realized, but their losses can only be used up to a maximum of $3,000 per year after gains have been offset.

For instance, an investor realizes $100,000 in short-term gains in a given year, and he is therefore responsible for $35,000 in tax. The following year, he loses $100,000, but he can only use $3,000 of that loss against other types of income, saving only $1,050 ($3000 x 35 percent) the following year. They can carry the loss forward, but it may take many years to realize the benefit.

GOOD NEWS/BAD NEWS OVERREACTIONS

To a certain extent, all investors react to good or bad news regarding the market. Investing gluttons, however, overreact. They are so hungry for action, they respond to the rumor of a merger or the hint of regulatory move by buying and selling. They become so worked up at the hint of bad news involving a stock they're holding that they reflexively sell; they become so eager for profit at possible good news that they immediately buy.

The irony is that these gluttons think they're getting a jump on the market, but in reality, they're lagging behind it. Stocks can often move before the first trade by 5 percent on good or bad news. As a result, investors that use good or bad news as a trigger for a trade usually are dealing with unfavorable price movement. They deceive themselves into thinking that by reacting quickly to a news report about a stock or a broader economic trend, they are going to get a jump on other investors. In reality, they are lagging behind the market as well as other investors who make less frequent but more strategic investing decisions.

Emotional investing based on good or bad market news is a hallmark of the rank amateur. Certainly some of these investments will pay off if a given stock responds logically—a piece of good news sends the stock on a sustained upward course, for instance. In many instances, however, logic is absent from market movement, especially in the short-term. The investing glutton moves so quickly that he never allows the long-term logic of the market to work for him.

The best long-term investors are savvy about big investment themes, and the four weaknesses just described prevent investing gluttons from developing this savvy. This doesn't mean that there isn't money to be made in daily transactions based on good and bad news, only that the glutton becomes so wrapped up in the daily news that he misses the long-term opportunities. For instance, consider the REIT (Real Estate Investment Trust) sector of the stock market. A REIT is a company that buys real estate and passes the net rental income through to the shareholders. Back in the beginning of 2000, you could buy a diversified REIT portfolio yielding nearly 8 percent. The stocks were generally trading at a discount to the underlying value of the real estate they held. If you held on to the REIT without doing a single trade or paying any commissions, you would have almost tripled your money five years later. A $10,000 investment on January 1, 2000, in a REIT index fund (such as Vanguard) would be worth $26,000 by December 2004 for an annualized return of around 21 percent.

It's highly unlikely that gluttons would tolerate a REIT's relative inaction, let alone an investment that they don't touch for five years. No doubt, if a glutton had made this investment, he would have jettisoned it at the first bad news in the REIT sector that resulted in a drop in prices—something that occurred a number of times over this five-year period. In addition, if an investor decided to sell the REIT at the end of five years, he would only be subject to a capital gains tax rate of 15 percent. Again, gluttons miss out on this lower capital gains rate.

Studies Reveal Gluttons Lose Money

If everything you've read up to this point describes your investing behaviors, you should also know that the simple remedy to this sin is trading less and enjoying it more. Reducing the frequency of trading may sound easy to those who aren't guilty of this sin, but to investing gluttons, it seems antithetical to their entire investing philosophy. If you're a glutton, you firmly believe that highly active trading is the key to success. If you want to stop being a glutton and stop losing money, then you should be aware of two studies that will disabuse you of your belief in hyperactive trading.

The first study was completed in 1998 by Brad M. Barber and Terrance Odean, professors at the graduate school of management at the

University of California at Davis. They examined the trading activity of 78,000 investors over a six-year period and found that the average investor turned over the stocks in his portfolio 80 percent annually, which may explain why individuals usually don't perform as well as the overall stock market. More significantly, Professors Barber and Odean broke down households into groups based on how frequently they turn over their portfolios. The low turnover group averaged just 1.5 percent turnover per year, meaning that they rarely traded out of stocks. The high turnover group had a 283 percent average annual turnover rate, meaning these investors change their entire portfolios three times a year. The average portfolio in the high turnover group delivered just a 10 percent annualized net return, while the low turnover group scored a market-beating 17.5 percent net return on average—these figures are without capital gains taxes, which if included would diminish the high turnover group's return even further.

A 2005 Morningstar Inc. study analyzed all U.S. stock funds' returns with ten-year records, focusing on the gap between the funds' official returns (what investors would have made if they stayed in the fund for the entire ten-year period) and the dollar-weighted returns for this period. To best explain the differences in stated vs. dollar-weighted returns, assume a mutual fund with $100 million in assets appreciates 20 percent in year one. In year two it has assets of $200 million and drops 20 percent. The stated return would be zero for the two-year period. Since the fund lost money while it had more assets the dollar-weighted return would be minus 11 percent. Among technology funds studied, the dollar-weighted returns lagged behind the stated returns by 14 percent. This suggests that investors rushed into the fund at its peak and pulled out at its low point. There was a smaller but still significant gap for other types of funds. The clear conclusion: People who left their money in funds for the full period did much better than people who became impatient and sold.

My experience tells me that these studies are right on the mark. I have heard one investor after the next justify their hyperactive trading by saying that they are increasing the odds of hitting a winner by investing all the time, and that this winner will more than compensate them for their losses. Theoretically, that is true. In reality, though, they tend to hit small winners and big losers. What they don't realize being a true investing player means being methodical and strategic rather than buying and selling as if one were in a race.

To help you become aware of your tendency to trade like there is no tomorrow, look at the following questions and see how many you answer affirmatively:

Do you feel like a day that goes by without making a trade is a day that has been wasted?

Are you convinced that the more trades you make, the more likely that one will come up a big winner?

Do you believe that by selling the moment a stock or fund starts moving south or even before that when negative news about a company surfaces, you are following a conservative strategy by limiting your losses?

Are you convinced that hyperactive trading is right for you (and perhaps wrong for others) because you're willing to invest time necessary to monitor your investments and change them at the first hint of trouble or opportunity?

Do you believe you are an excellent investor because of your frequent trades, even though your portfolio performance doesn't reflect excellence?

Have you found that you have a tendency to be overly optimistic about good-performing stocks and overly pessimistic about ones that don't perform well?

Have you held any stock or fund in your portfolio for more than a year; are you more likely to keep something less than a year; less than six months?

Do you favor investments with a lot of action, ones with the highest potential for gain; do you eschew investments with little action and only modest potential for short-term gain?

The more "yes" answers you have, the more vigilant you need to be against the sin of gluttony.

Put Yourself on an Investing Diet

The good news about this investing sin is that you have a number of ways to reduce its negative impact. Here are some steps you can take to reduce your gluttony and find a more healthy balance between active trading and watchful waiting:

1. ***Reserve 5 to 10 percent of your portfolio for aggressive trading.*** Just as a diet isn't designed to eliminate all food—or even all junky food—a good regimen for the investing glutton isn't to cut trading entirely. For whatever reason, you enjoy and need the action of buying and selling. What you don't need is for this need to eat away at your portfolio. Therefore, reserve a small percentage to feed this habit. If you only actively trade 100 shares instead of 1,000, you probably won't do much damage.

Remember, though, that this 10 percent high-end percentage is absolute! Invariably, a time will come when the actively traded 10 percent will be performing well, and the inner glutton's voice will say, "Don't be a sucker; you're a much better investor now than before; up the percentage to 20 percent." Do not heed this voice. It is the same voice the dieter hears after losing ten pounds, the voice that says, "Another slice of chocolate cake won't hurt you."

2. ***Limit your active trading to an IRA or some other tax-deferred account.*** This can include a company 401(k) if allowed or an IRA rollover from a previous employer; the rollover can often be transferred to a discount brokerage account from the custodian of your former employer. Obviously, limiting your active trading to tax-deferred accounts will help you avoid paying big short-term capital gains taxes.

3. ***Refuse to invest in the stocks and funds that everyone is talking about.*** I recognize that this is going to be difficult advice to follow. For a glutton, especially, it will feel counterintuitive. You hear the "buy" recommendations, notice a strong earnings report, read stories lauding a company's future, and your impulse is to strike while the iron is hot. As we've indicated, however, the iron is already starting to cool when you make your buying decision. The stock that is rated a "buy" by 20 out of 21 brokerage firms has great expectations already built into its price; the majority of people have already discovered and bought it, and the odds are against a significant number of additional people flocking to the stock and helping further inflate its price.

Gluttons who want to keep their vow not to chase performance should keep eBay in mind. Since going public in 1998 until the end of 2004, eBay's stock price rose thirty fold from its IPO. In a very average year for equities in 2004, eBay rose 80 percent. The P/E ratio was over fifty times 2005 earnings estimates. Despite all this, buying eBay at the start of 2005 would have been a mistake. Even though it has consistently received "buy" ratings and exceeded earnings estimates, it was tapped out from an investing standpoint. After missing the earning estimate by 2 cents for the first quarter of 2004, eBay gave back nearly the entire appreciation in price of 2004 in the first six months of 2005.

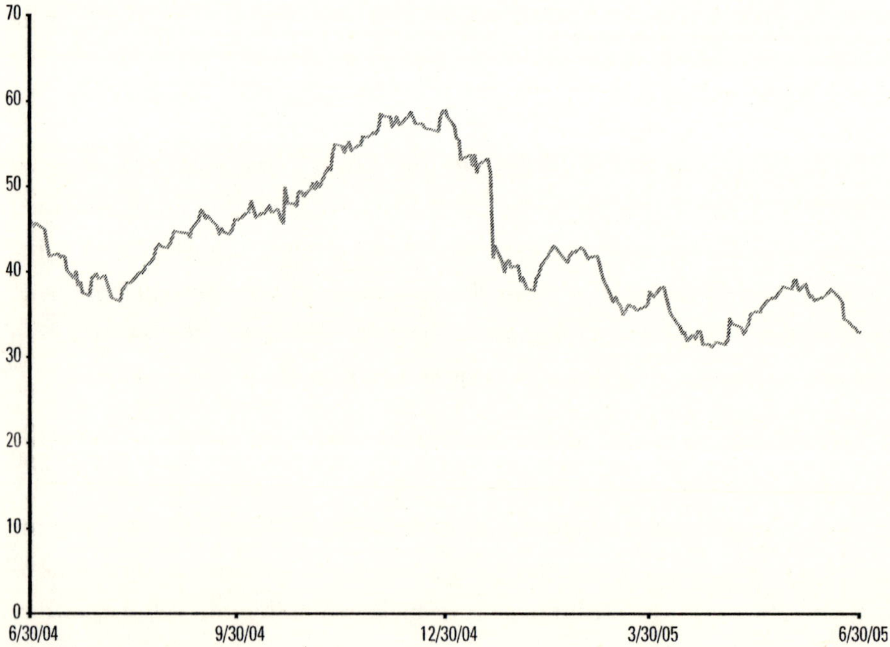

eBay: 6/30/2004–6/30/2005

To stop chasing performance, here are some warning signs to heed:

— The majority of brokerage firms have issued "buy" recommendations

— A big story appears in a major business publication lauding a company's performance and future prospects

— A stock or fund's price has consistently been going up for more than a year

— The high performance of a stock has you saying to yourself, "I wish I would have bought that ___ years ago."

— More than one friend or colleague tells you about the stock or fund they invested in, its great performance and how you should get in on the action.

4. ***Substitute buying "beaten up" stocks for high-performing ones.*** To satisfy your craving for action, look toward solid stocks that have taken a beating. In other words, find a company that has a stellar reputation, a history of good performance, and other outstanding attributes, but for one reason or another has experienced problems that have depressed the stock price. Obviously, you don't want to choose Enron-like companies that have committed fatal or near-fatal blunders, but ones that have been hurt by forces beyond their control. Every organization runs into bad luck now and then; every company fails to seize an opportunity or commits an anomalous mistake. If you can find the window when the price has fallen lower than it should be—when the market has overreacted to negative events involving the company—then this is the moment when your impulse for action can serve you well.

Ideally, you want to find a stock like Merck & Co. After the company announced the withdrawal of Vioxx on September 30, 2004, the stock fell from $45 to $33 per share in one day. It fell another $7 to $25.60 over the following six weeks due to litigation concerns. When the stock went below $30, many brokerage firms changed their rating from "buy" to "sell."

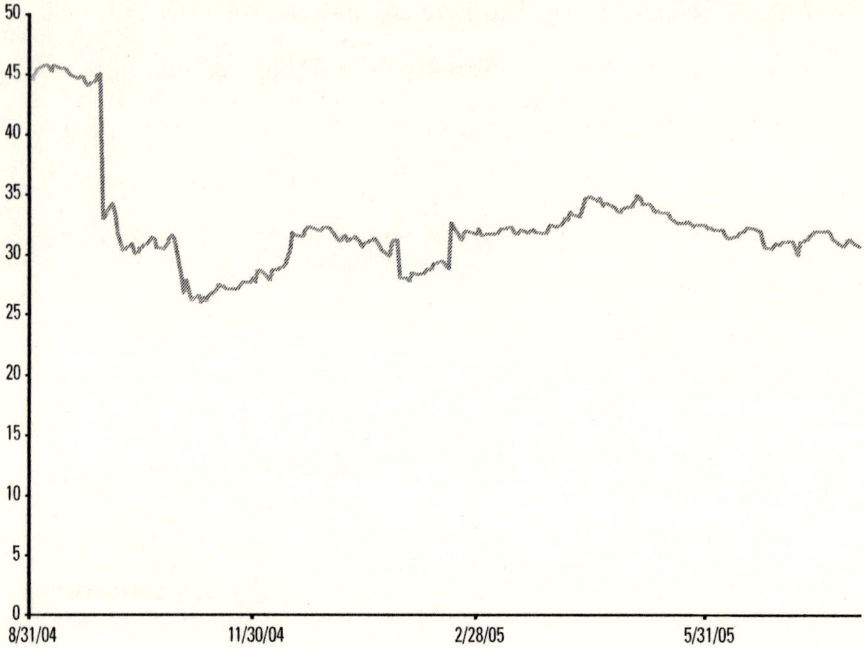

Merck: 8/31/2004–7/31/2005

In November, when Merck was at its nadir, the stock yielded almost 6 percent. The P/E ratio was at 10, and relatively few people were interested in purchasing the stock. The stock was off 45 percent from its 52-week high at this time, making it a wise buy for savvy investors. Merck met the qualifications I described earlier—it was a strong company with a great tradition and history of highly profitable products. Merck could not be blamed for the research revealing the dangers of taking Vioxx. It was an anomaly and not indicative of the effort they made to create safe, useful pharmaceuticals. This is not to say that significant litigation issues are not a concern for the stock in the future, but they seem to be largely priced into the stock. Apparently the market recognized this fact, since by 2006 Merck had recovered to $35 per share.

Gluttons like action and movement; they like the sense of being a player and finding hot stocks. By investing in companies like Merck that have taken a hit, they can satisfy these needs without taking the same types of risks as they would on a high-flyer. Certain investing gluttons have to be careful and not back a stock that is down and is never going to recover. They also must recognize that buying a stock like Merck is tricky, since no one is quite sure how deep the bottom is, and they may have to weather further downward movements in price before it goes up. Still, I've found that looking for beat-up stocks is a far better strategy for gluttons than looking for high-performing ones.

5. ***Increase benchmarking.*** Every investing glutton should make a practice of comparing their portfolio's performance with various market benchmarks, such as the S&P 500, NASDAQ Composite, or the Russell 2000. Doing this comparison once a month is a reality check of sorts. Too many gluttons view their investing performance through rose-colored glasses, and therefore feel no motivation to change how they invest. I would bet that the vast majority of gluttons perform below the market benchmarks. If this is the case, this monthly measurement will serve as motivation to change their overactive strategy.

6. ***Reduce the number of trades gradually.*** Don't immediately try and go from five investments a day to one a week. You'll find this radical transition tough to maintain. Instead, diminish your trades incrementally. Go from five trades a day to one or two a day. Then in a few weeks, reduce this number to three or four trades weekly. If you find this rate tolerable, try and moving down to one trade a week. You don't have to be rigid in this discipline—if two great investment opportunities arise in a given week, you should capitalize on them. You should, however, keep track of the number of trades you make and your ability to reduce their number and maintain that reduced number over time.

7. ***Use a passive or index strategy when investing in small caps.*** I am tempted to recommend that investing gluttons avoid small caps altogether, since they can eat up an overactive investor's money with great speed. At the same time, I recognize that gluttons are drawn to small caps and that they can offer a better return than large company stocks, especially when they are held for a significant period of time. According to Ibbotson

Associates, over the 79-year period between 1925 and 2004, small company stocks have outperformed large ones by 2.3 percent per year.

If, however, you are tempted to be an active investor in small caps, recognize that this superior performance probably won't apply to you. Because there are thousands of stocks in this sector, you need to be extraordinarily knowledgeable and vigilant about which ones you pick. Even the average stockbroker is ill-prepared to handle small caps effectively. It takes a fund manager who does little else but small caps to navigate all the minefields in this area.

A passive or index strategy provides a much better alternative. You can purchase an exchange-traded fund such as the Russell 2000 iShares, which trade under the ticker IWM. This holds a basket of the smaller 2000 of the Russell 3000 index. The fund carries a modest expense ratio of only .20 percent annually. During a period of poor returns for the average equity investor, this fund produced an average annual return of 7.25 percent during its first five years of trading (from 2000 to 2005).

Use Energy Wisely

Gluttons may not have a lot of patience, but they have energy to burn. As you may have guessed from reading about the traits of gluttons or if you are guilty of this sin yourself, these individuals are manic in their investing. They eat, sleep, and breathe investments. They spend a lot of time and mental energy weighing their various options and engaging in internal debates about what to do. They also love talking investing, not only with other investors and professionals but with anyone who will tolerate their obsession. They also spend a great deal of time on their trades, exploring esoteric stocks and funds and immersing themselves in the technical details.

Not all of this is bad, but ultimately, a significant amount of their energy is misdirected. Therefore, here are some ways that investing gluttons can put their considerable amount of energy to better and more profitable use:

➜ Research investments before making them. This may not be as exciting as doing an actual trade or talking with a professional, but it can be a much more productive use of your time. Spend less time trading and more time figuring out what trades make the most sense. Information tends to have a "sedating" effect on overactive investors. The more they learn, the more conservative they become.

➜ Make an effort to spend free time on noninvesting activities. The best investors will tell you they need to get away from the business regularly in order to think clearly about it and gain perspective on it. If you go home from work and go online and do research and trade in the aftermarket for hours, you will have no perspective and view investing like a rank amateur. Therefore, force yourself to go on vacations, spend time with your family, take up a new hobby, and the like. In other words, take your mind off investing periodically so when you come back to it, you'll do so with a clear mind.

➜ Concentrate your energy on a smaller number of trades. Gluttons tend to disperse their energy over numerous investments. They spend a little time and effort on each one, which may add up to a lot, but it's not focused energy. When you're considering an investment, consider it seriously. This means doing your homework, talking to pros and giving yourself some time to reflect on the advisability of moving forward. As we suggested earlier, investing gluttons need to learn discipline, and one great way of doing so is by expending more energy in a focused way on a relatively small number of investments.

8

Sloth

The Cost of Being Lazy

Sloth comes with the investing territory. Even investing gluttons can be slothful at times, obsessive in some investing areas and neglectful in others. Most investors, though, don't view themselves as lazy or sinfully negligent. Instead, they rationalize their sloth. Some people place too much trust in an advisor and tell themselves that they don't have to watch their investments because their advisor is watching them. Others don't bother doing much research before buying or selling an investment, convinced that they can never learn enough to make much of a difference. Still others do their homework in one investing area but ignore their responsibilities in others—they find it interesting and exciting to research potential investments but find it boring to monitor investment performance and the larger market regularly.

Sloth is also a sin of varying degrees. Some people are extraordinarily, consistently lazy about their investing while others are only fitfully slothful. I have known investors who have done a pretty good job of doing their pre-investing research and keeping track of their investments for a period of time and then become neglectful and make serious, costly mistakes. In fact, some people who do well in the market may start out by being vigilant investors and then, because of their success, become overly confident, less vigilant, and even sloppy.

Therefore, to help you define slothful investing and determine how much of a sinner you are in this area, we need to look at the sin on a continuum.

From a Little Lazy to a Complete Slug

On a sloth continuum, the following four points exist: A little lazy, Erratically engaged, Generally disinterested, A complete slug. As you read the description of each, see if you can spot yourself on the continuum.

A LITTLE LAZY

These types of investors spend time on their portfolios, reviewing monthly statements and having a good idea about asset allocation. They know most of the securities they own, and they generally don't make investments on whims—they want to do some research before they make an investing commitment.

At times, they don't pay attention to individual stocks in their portfolio, content with a general overview of performance. They also tend to take their mutual fund holdings for granted, failing to do regular assessments in order to determine if it's time to sell them. It's not unusual for these investors to overlook poor earnings announcements when the price of a stock is holding up. For more diligent investors, this might be an excellent selling opportunity. In the same way, they may not pay attention to a stock that has doubled the dividend, resulting in a dramatic increase in its price. They may sell this stock prematurely, even though the yield is much more attractive with the dividend increase.

All in all, somewhat lazy investors do a decent job of monitoring their investments, and their sloth may hurt them every so often, but not to the extent that it makes a big dent in their portfolio.

ERRATICALLY ENGAGED

These investors pay attention to their portfolios and the market, but they don't do so consistently. They may research a fund in one instance, and the next time simply follow the recommendation of a friend or advisor without doing any research at all. They open their monthly brokerage reports, but they are as likely to give them a cursory glance as to peruse them thoroughly. Unlike the investor who is a little lazy, they tend to be more hit and miss. They might catch big news such as takeovers or scandals related to stocks they hold, but they often don't pay attention to lesser news.

By being erratically engaged, these investors are erratically successful. Or, put another way, their occasional sloth makes them vulnerable to silly, easily preventable mistakes. A little bit of laziness is to be expected. When laziness and vigilance are split 50/50, though, sloth can take a significant chunk out of a portfolio.

GENERALLY DISINTERESTED

If the previous point on the continuum represented a 50/50 split between sloth and vigilance, this point is more like 75/25. They may pay attention after they realize they've suffered a significant downturn or when they're considering a major change in their portfolio, but the majority of the time they are apathetic. For instance, they invest in mutual funds but have no idea of what the funds' objectives are. If you ask them whether their fund buys large-cap growth or emerging markets, they probably can't tell you. They may even pay a load (a sales commission as high as 5 percent) to purchase a mutual fund because they haven't done their homework and realize they have better options. These investors also leave their brokerage statements in their envelopes, and when they purchase a stock, they may not review the holding for months.

It may take significant bad news to get them to pay attention and sell, and it may also require a broker, advisor, or friend making a convincing argument before they seize an investment opportunity. While they may respond to extremes and do their homework and take action in the face of extremely good or bad news, they generally remain phlegmatic investors at other times. As a result, they are unable to take advantage of the trends and unable to get out of bad investments before it has cost them a pretty penny.

A COMPLETE SLUG

These people view investing the way they do plumbing; they wash their hands of the responsibility. Either they blindly follow an advisor or some other guru, or they take a fatalistic approach and believe that investing is a crap shoot so why waste energy on research or analysis. In either case, these individuals only look at their investment reports when they gather material to give to their accountants at year's end. They have little idea how their mutual funds perform from year to year and only think about investments when their broker suggests they buy or sell (and they make a decision primarily based on their broker's recommendation). They are vaguely aware of how the market is doing but don't follow it, claiming to have little interest in its ups and downs. If they work for a company, they may not even know if they participate in their company's 401(k) plans and if they do, how their investments are allocated. In fact, they may be too lazy to take advantage of tax-deferred vehicles such as 401(k) plans. Some of these extremely sluggish investors are sluggish because they are "investing snobs"; they see the machinations of the market and associated investing responsibilities as beneath them. Others are naively trusting in their brokers. Still others have had a number of bad investments, became frustrated with their poor decisions, and decided that they were no longer interested in active participation in the process.

This extreme sloth can result in serious losses and major missed opportunities. They become sitting ducks for unscrupulous stockbrokers who come to them with bad IPOs or new issue closed-end funds with imbedded 6 percent sales commission for the initial buyer. They also take no initiative to capitalize on information they pick up or ask their advisors for recommendations. They are the ultimate passive investors, allowing the market to take them in whatever direction it wants. More often than not, this passive stance causes them to stick with investments too long or to sell them at the worst possible times.

As you consider where on the continuum you're located, be aware that most people don't fall squarely on point 1, 2, 3, or 4. Instead, they exist somewhere in between the points and their slothfulness varies over time. In certain situations—when they are stressed out from work or in other areas of their lives—they may be more slothful. The goal is to locate your approximate location on the continuum and recognize that it's not a fixed point but one that can move around a bit.

Another way to figure out your slothful quotient is by placing check marks next to any of the following statements that apply to you:

__ Fail to review brokerage or mutual fund statements regularly

__ Have no idea what the investment objectives of your mutual fund are

__ Rarely review company news and information for stocks you hold

__ Have no clue about imbedded loads or sales commissions of investments you buy from brokers

__ Lack knowledge of historic relative performance of a mutual fund holding or whether the expense ratio is appropriate or too high

__ Unaware of your asset allocation

__ Pay little or no attention to benefits of tax-deferred vehicles or take advantage of company-matching investments

__ Do a poor job keeping track of investing paperwork and where investments are held

__ Make investments based on little or no due diligence

Scoring:

0–2 Checks: A little lazy

3–5 Checks: Erratically engaged

6–7 Checks: Generally disinterested

8–9 Checks: A complete slug

Profile of a Sloth

Phil is a sloth in the middle of the continuum, a successful salesperson with a large pharmaceutical company who must put in a lot of hours on the road as part of his job. Because he spends a good deal of time away from home, he relishes every moment that he can spend with his family—his wife and two small children. As a result of this vow, Phil rarely does any work at home; he also refrains from doing anything involving his investments. Although he has plenty of time to look at investment statements or talk to his broker when he's waiting for planes in airports or when he has dead time in hotel rooms, Phil usually avoids these tasks. To him, it's just more work, and he figures he works hard enough as it is.

The only time Phil really engages in investing is when a work colleague notes a trend in the pharmaceutical industry and suggests an investment that capitalizes on that trend. In these moments, Phil realizes that a certain type of investment makes sense, and he calls his broker to discuss it. At times during the year, Phil's broker will call him with an interesting investment. In most instances, Phil won't call his broker back immediately or avoids thinking or making a decision about his broker's recommendation for a very long time. Not that he is researching it on his own or seeking other opinions; he is just being lazy. On more than one occasion, Phil has missed following the recommendation of his broker after wasting valuable days or even weeks putting off a decision because he can't carve out the time necessary to study the investment recommendation. Sometimes after a period of time passes and Phil still hasn't studied it, he simply tells his broker to go ahead and buy it. Other times, he does his due diligence. In both cases, though, Phil has wasted so much time due to his sloth that he invariably doesn't reap as much of the investing reward as he would have if he had done his homework immediately and made a decision at that earlier point.

Like many slothful investors, Phil rationalizes his sloth. He convinces himself that no matter how much he learns about investing or how diligently he monitors his portfolio, he won't have much impact on the portfolio's performance. Or rather, he believes that the impact would be negligible, so why spend a lot of precious time on this task? In Phil's mind, his investing sin makes perfect sense. He thinks that friends and colleagues who read every investment statement they receive, who study the market, who subscribe to newsletter, and who check their portfolio's performance online have misplaced priorities. Phil would rather spend time with his family or playing golf than spend it poring over a statement.

What Phil doesn't understand is that this is not an either-or choice. The options are not to be an investing glutton or a slothful one. There is a middle ground that avoids either sin. Phil, though, avoids this middle ground in large part because he feels that by trusting his broker to do the right thing, he doesn't have to do much of anything. As we'll see, this is the most common trap that slothful investors fall into.

Ceding Control to Someone Else

If you're a slothful sinner, you're going to look for ways to minimize how much time and energy you expend on investing. This may make perfect sense to you since you devalue investing activities and tell yourself that someone else is more qualified to handle them, but what you're really doing is being an irresponsible investor. You're essentially saying, "I don't want to think about my investments; I don't want to talk about them. I just want to put my money in some good stocks and bonds and then not worry about it." Without long-term goals, oversight responsibility or a desire to learn about the subject, you might as well put all your money in a savings account and be done with it. If, like most people, you are investing with an eye toward retirement, a child's college education, or some other significant expenditure down the road, you must have some involvement in the investing process. Your degree of involvement can vary based on your interest level, type of investing you choose, and other factors, but you can't delegate all responsibility away. At a minimum, monitor your broker or advisor and make sure your returns are appropriate for the amount of risk you are taking and how the market is performing.

Slothful investors, however, delegate all or most of this responsibility. They may turn everything over to their broker and eschew all involvement.

They may depend completely on a media guru for investing advice and follow it without doing any homework or monitoring their investments. They may read one article or book, decide they know everything they need to know, and never read anything else. They are looking for the easiest, least time-consuming investing method, and one way or another, they're going to find easy doesn't mean successful.

A common reflex of slothful investors is to rely exclusively on a single newsletter or other source of information for investing knowledge. For people who are lazy about choosing investments, this seems like an ideal alternative. They invest unwarranted value on a single source of information and recommendations and follow it unwaveringly. It doesn't take much time, and it reassures them that they've placed their money in better hands than their own. When I worked at Salomon Brothers, some of my colleagues relied exclusively on the *Gilder Technology Newsletter* for their investment ideas. When tech holdings were going strong, this was fine, but when tech collapsed in 2000 and 2001, these colleagues suffered enormous losses.

It's fine to find and read a favorite newsletter or listen to a Wall Street pundit on the radio who seems to be very smart, but you don't want to limit your knowledge to one or even two sources. Savvy investors incorporate a variety of investing newsletters and other reports into the mix. They recognize that if they rely on only one, they will likely receive a distorted perspective of the market. My colleagues who were so reliant on the *Gilder Newsletter* may have been able to identify the coming tech downswing if they made the effort to read other newsletters or had a handle on the outrageous valuations of the stock they held.

Slothful investors also place inordinate faith in their brokers, assuming that they will do all the work and make better recommendations than they could arrive at on their own. While some brokers are extremely smart about the market and highly ethical, not all are. In fact, for every good broker, you'll find a bad one. Those odds should scare most people, but they don't have much of an effect on slothful investors. They don't realize that some brokers are primarily interested in selling high margin product to generate fat commissions. For example, Steve found a broker who came highly recommended, and he entrusted him with $1 million and the authority to invest the money as he saw fit. Steve, an extremely successful attorney, enjoyed his clients' complete trust when handling their affairs, and he saw no reason that he should not give a broker the same respect. In addition, Steve had little time to spend on investing. As a litigator in a large law firm responsible for high-profile class action suits, Steve was up to his eyeballs in work. He had accumulated a sizable bank account over the years, and his friends and wife had been after him to invest the money rather than keep most of it in the safe certificate of deposits that his bank offered. When this broker was recommended to Steve, he thought all his problems had been solved. During the first few months of their relationship, the market was good, and most of the broker's trades increased the value of the portfolio. Steve paid no attention to what the broker did, allowing him complete freedom to make whatever trades he wanted. When a colleague pointed out to Steve that the broker earned commissions on each trade and that provided an incentive to "churn" the account, Steve said he really didn't care as long as the portfolio kept increasing in value.

Of course, it started decreasing in value, and because of Steve's sloth, he didn't fire the broker until he had lost over $400,000.

The lesson here is not to turn your account over to a broker who works on commission, especially if you have slothful tendencies. If you wish to use a broker, find someone who will charge a reasonable fee based on the asset value. In this way, the broker makes more money only when he increases the account value. Still, slothful investors should take some responsibility for overseeing what is happening with their money. They don't have to be aware of all the details in each trade or call their broker constantly for updates and information, but they should monitor activity regularly. This is the only way to know if brokers are doing a good job and execute an early escape if they aren't.

What I should stress above all else, though, is that if sloth applies to your investing pattern, you should beware of trusting any one source of advice or information. I know investors who rely exclusively on an investing columnist or make an investment as soon as they hear an analyst recommendation. A single source may save you time and effort, but it also is likely to be inaccurate. While some investment pundits are knowledgeable, they also frequently publish their recommendations too late—to take full advantage of them, the investor would have had to act days, weeks, or even months earlier.

Perhaps the biggest misconception slothful investors have is that analysts can point them toward consistently strong investments; that all they have to do is pay attention to analysts, act on their recommendations, and they can sit back and count their money. In reality, analysts' recommendations to buy, sell, or hold aren't much different from the earnings guidance companies provide. They can be useful, but only when looked at within a larger context.

Before relying exclusively on analysts, you should also be aware that analysts are extremely fallible. Certainly there are good ones, but there are also analysts who are unethical—who recommend investing in companies because they want to receive investment banking business from those companies. Perhaps just as disturbing, some analysts favor stocks that have experienced a great run or downgrade stocks after all the bad news is priced in. If you just follow this analyst's advice, you'll come too late to the party and stay too long; you'll buy a stock after its had most of its run and you'll sell it after it's already gone down a lot.

Given all this, slothful investors should rouse themselves out of their lethargic investing states and gather information from diverse sources before making decisions. They should also monitor their investing performance regularly.

Time and Sloth: Putting in the Hours Appropriate for Your Investing Mode

Sloth is often a function of time. It may be that you don't have the hours or don't want to put in the hours necessary to be a good investor. That's fine. Though there is a minimum amount of work every investor needs to do, you must find the right investing mode given the hours you are willing to expend. Your sloth may result from being in the wrong mode; you're trying to do it yourself when you really should be relying on a money manager. The three modes, therefore, are:

- Doing it yourself
- Focusing on mutual funds
- Using a money manager

If you do it yourself, you need to make the time commitment to do it right. This doesn't have to be a huge commitment, but an hour or two weekly is probably the least you can get away with. If you're not spending that time, you're being slothful, and you will pay for your inattention to your investments. If you lack the time or the interest to do it yourself, and have only chosen this mode because you want to save money on commissions and management fees, then you should consider switching to one of the other two modes where the time requirements are less.

Mutual funds require less time, but you still need to do your homework to pick the right fund for you, taking into consideration their track records as well as the fees they charge. You also need to monitor their performance and be prepared to switch if necessary.

Using a money manager is the least time-intensive alternative, but as I noted earlier, you can't simply turn everything over to a broker or advisor and assume he will manage your investments like they were his own. You still must monitor what he does and how well he performs versus other money managers to get a sense of his value. Even if you find the perfect money manager and have absolute faith in his abilities, you must spend one or two hours every quarter reviewing what has been done.

Of course, some people don't choose just one of these investing modes but use them in different combinations. For instance, you might use a money manager for some investments but invest on your own for others. Whatever your particular choice is, determine if you're putting in the hours necessary to avoid sloth. To make this determination, answer the following questions:

— Do you spend no more than an hour or two per month (and often less) monitoring your investments?

— When you do find time to look at your statements, do you find yourself distracted and not really concentrating on what you're reading?

— Do you find yourself thinking that you should evaluate how your assets are allocated and do other investment tasks but other things to distract you and you never get around to it?

— Does it seem as if you have a short attention span when it comes to your investments; are you unable to spend more than a few minutes doing your investing homework before your mind starts drifting?

— Do you start analyzing your investments or your advisor then stop as you rationalize that you don't know what you're doing and you're just wasting time?

Answering yes to at least some of these questions suggests that you need to refocus your time when it comes to investing. As you'll discover, just making a commitment to do so isn't enough. What you really need is a routine.

Fighting Lethargy and Inaction: Establish a New Routine

Lazy and indifferent investors need to force themselves to pay attention to their investments. If they just tell themselves that they'll try and pay more attention, they are likely to fail. Typically, a slothful investor will experience an investing loss and vow to pay more attention and become more diligent. He may even make an effort to do so for a while, but the odds are that he'll slip back into his old behaviors if his investments return to their normal performance. Investing laziness is a habit that's tough to break, which is why my recommendation is to establish a new routine.

Here are the behaviors that you should incorporate into this routine:

1. SET UP AN E-MAIL ALERT

If you are managing your money yourself and buying individual stocks, this e-mail alert will automatically and regularly provide you with the earnings release of the companies you own. I monitor my personal holdings through a Yahoo! Finance page that tracks all my stocks and allows me to view headlines and news stories from the *Wall Street Journal, Dow Jones,* and other financial publications.

2. REVIEW YOUR MONTHLY STATEMENT WITH A SHARP EYE FOR CHANGES.

A slothful glance at a monthly financial statement is worthless. What you need to do is review it and be alert for any significant changes. Has the market price moved up or down in dramatic fashion? If so, see if you can trace this movement to news or an event that triggered this movement. Then ask yourself if the cause of the change makes you more or less inclined to hold the stock or if an opportunity exists to add to your position.

Similarly, look at your asset allocation and determine if some event has shifted the balance. Perhaps you had a bond mature and the money is sitting in cash. Maybe equities rallied hard in the quarter and they now compose an inordinately large percentage of your portfolio.

3. EVALUATE YOUR MUTUAL FUND OR ADVISOR RELATIVE TO THE MARKET OR OTHER STANDARDS.

In other words, determine how your mutual fund did versus the average mutual fund in the same category or how your advisor did compared to a well-publicized market index. Make this determination based on several time horizons such as the quarter, year, and a multiyear period. This way you'll get a sense if you're doing good, bad, or average. For instance, in a quarter where most broad market indices are up 5 percent and your portfolio went down 5 percent something is horribly wrong and you need to investigate further. It may be that your advisor is too aggressive and bought speculative stocks that did not rise with the rally. It may be that your mutual funds went down 20 percent, but that this is a correction after they rose more than 30 percent in the previous three quarters; that this mutual fund volatility is in line with other, similar types of mutual funds. If you're keeping track of this performance quarterly and comparing it to other, similar funds (or the performance of other advisors) on a quarterly basis, you will have the information you need to make smart decisions.

In addition to incorporating these behaviors into your routine, designate a specific time and day for each of them. Determine a daily or weekly time when you will look at your e-mail alert; identify when you're going to set aside thirty minutes or so each month to review your statements; figure out when you can spend an hour or two evaluating and comparing your mutual fund and advisor performance to the market. Mark these dates and times on a calendar and stick to them. At first you're going to have to make a conscious effort to incorporate them into your routine, but after a while, they will become habit and help you manage your slothful tendencies.

Sloth Can Take Many Forms

Unlike our other deadly sins, sloth is a sin of omission rather than of commission. For this reason, it is more difficult to identify, categorize, and prevent. Sloth manifests itself in many different ways, but its manifestation involves laziness, forgetfulness, procrastination, and rationalization. In other words, it takes the form of thought rather than action. The routine described in the previous section will be a good preventative step against sloth, but you can still follow the routine and not be as involved in your investing as you should be or as willing to take action when action needs to be taken. For instance, just because you're aware your mutual fund is not performing as well as the industry average over a sustained period of time doesn't mean that you'll investigate other funds, take your money out of one and put it in a better-performing one. You can still just sit on your assets and say to yourself, "Oh well, it's bound to do better next quarter."

To help you avoid falling into the slothful trap, I'm going to describe three different investors guilty of sloth and how this sin affected their investing. Then, I'm going to suggest the specific actions you should take if you find yourself following the same paths as these investors:

"At first glance, Bob doesn't seem like a slothful investor. Beginning in the early 1980s, Bob started putting aside $1,000 monthly in CDs that were earning 9 percent to save for his kids' college education as well as retirement. He had done a lot of homework about CD rates in his area and found a bank that offered the highest rate. During this time, Bob avoided bonds and equities, content with his return and having done the math—he knew he'd be in great shape if he continued saving $1,000 every month, even if the rate dropped a bit. Every time he received a CD statement from the bank, Bob would read it carefully and be pleased with how his money was growing. When he would roll over his CDs annually, he saw that rates were dropping, but at this point he had accumulated a sizable sum of money, and he didn't want to endanger it by investing in a riskier vehicle. As the rates continued to drop, Bob continued to rationalize his strategy and failed to gather information that would have shot holes in his rationalization. For instance, if Bob had conducted even a little bit of research, he might have discovered that between 1926 and 2004, equities have always provided a positive return over every overlapping 15-year period, and since these funds were for college, some equity weighting would have been appropriate. In fact, equities rallied 13.2 percent per annum and long-term bonds appreciated 10.8 percent between 1984 and 2004 (according to Ibbotson Associates). If Bob had invested his $12,000 in stocks in 1984, that investment alone would have been worth $143,000 in 2004. Because Bob was unaware of these and similar historical numbers, he lost hundreds of thousands of dollars that a conservative but more balanced portfolio would have netted. Although Bob was diligent about saving, initially found a good rate by doing research, and monitored his statements, he still was slothful. His myopic focus on his CDs prevented him from looking at other investments that would have provided a much greater return during the twenty years."

If Bob's slothful traits seem similar to your own, make sure you broaden your knowledge about the investing world and what is going on in the market. Some simple statistics may jar you out of your happily ignorant approach and cause you to take action. Do a little bit of research about different types of investments that aren't in your portfolio and market trends over time for these investments. Then compare them with the return for your particular investment type. If you seem to be missing out—as Bob missed out on one of the biggest equity and bond rallies of the century—you might be motivated to reallocate your investment funds.

On our sloth continuum, Bob was erratically engaged. Our next example, Pam, is a complete slug.

> "In 1989 Pam entrusted her entire portfolio to her brother-in-law, a broker at a major brokerage firm. Pam, a doctor, made a good living and periodically added cash to the portfolio. She found everything about investing boring, though, so she gave her brother-in-law complete discretion over the account. She didn't even know what she placed in the account. Still, Pam knew it was prudent to open the statements she received from him, and in the early part of the 1990s, she read the statements and saw that her balance was growing, though it was growing slowly and steadily rather than by leaps and bounds. Pam had no idea what he was investing her money in—she skipped over that part of the statement—and was content that the account was growing. After 1995, she stopped opening the statements and just stacked them in a shoebox in her closet. She trusted him—he was her brother-in-law, after all—and knew he had her best interests at heart. What Pam didn't know was that the broker was placing her in mutual funds with high loads that also carried high expense ratios. He also bought new issue closed-end bond funds with 5 percent gross commissions. In 2002 she finally had her brother-in-law (the broker) calculate how much cash she had invested with him. It was merely equal to the value of the portfolio 13 years later."

If you're like Pam, the obvious recommendation is to open and read your statements regularly and compare them with market averages. Less obviously, perhaps, make appointments to talk with brokers once or twice a year, especially in person. Come armed with the statements and the comparisons, and feel free to question them about their strategy and rationale for it. It may well be that they are worthy of your trust, but if you communicate your involvement and awareness of what is going on with your portfolio, you may protect yourself against ethically challenged brokers. When brokers know that you're vigilant and informed, they are much less likely to think they can churn an account. And if they are honest, then they will appreciate your interest and questions and will feel even more motivated to do well by you.

"Harry, a law firm partner, avoided stocks and bonds entirely, preferring direct investments such as real estate deals and venture capital that made him feel like an insider. His clients, real estate companies, and other entrepreneurial concerns, often told him about these direct investments and invited him to participate. Harry did so gladly, loving the excitement of being part of ventures such as these. He liked passing by a shopping center that was being built and telling friends that he had invested in it. Though Harry liked hearing about the upside of these ventures and had a lawyer's appreciation of the risk and reward scenarios, he was bored by the details. He figured that because he considered himself an "insider," the majority of the deals would pay off handsomely and compensate him for the ones that didn't. Therefore, Harry did what he would never do with a law firm client—he failed to study the details involving cash flow, company histories, and so on. Harry was far from a lazy person—he was one of the hardest working partners at his law firm—but a lot of the fun for him was just knowing about the big picture and other prominent people who were also investors. Studying all the details and keeping informed of developments struck Harry as too much like what he did for a living. To Harry, these direct investments were fun. Though Harry never lost a lot of money investing in this lazy manner, he also didn't make much. It was a zero-sum game, and Harry would have made a lot more money if he had simply put all his money in conservative mutual funds available to everyone."

You may not be like Harry in the sense that you feel you're an insider and only invest in insider ventures, but you may possess a similarly elitist attitude that causes you to ignore the details. Since this is a book about the seven deadly sins, it seems appropriate to note that the devil is in the details when it comes to investing. Be lazy about learning the nitty-gritty facts of an investment—its performance in the past, a company's earnings, and so on—and you place yourself at a tremendous disadvantage relative to investors who do know the details. I have encountered investors who enjoy dropping the names of investment books they have read and esoteric investing techniques they have mastered, but these people's investments generally don't perform as well as expected because they ignore crucial facts. They invest in what they are sure will become a hot internet security company because they are working on a new technology, but they fail to look at the company's financial condition and learn that their existence is precarious. Therefore, if you're like Harry, spend a little extra time and familiarize yourself with the boring details as well as the exciting big picture.

9

Sinful Situations

Be Aware of Events and Environments That Tempt Investors

Certain situations make sinful investing behavior more likely than others. You may find that you're able to resist sloth, gluttony, or any of the other sins by following the advice in these pages, but under special circumstances, you forget everything you've learned and fall back into old sinful investing patterns. The good news is that this can be prevented if you're aware of the situations that cause you problems and know what to do when you find yourself enmeshed in them.

Therefore, let's look at these situations, starting with ones involving inside information.

So Much of an Insider That You Can't Get Out

Inside information is almost always an intoxicating myth, and it is especially intoxicating to investors vulnerable to all seven sins.

For the slothful investor, inside information is the perfect shortcut. It promises easy money with little effort. For someone who is lazy about investing and wants to make the process as simple as possible, inside information seems to be the perfect solution.

For the greedy investor, inside information holds out the promise of riches. He wants to believe in whatever tip he receives because it allows him to dream about the vast fortune that will soon be his.

For the envious investor, this is a chance to show everyone that he too can outperform the market. He daydreams about how a bit of inside information will give him the huge win that has escaped him in the past, and finally he will be the envy of others rather than vice versa.

For the lustful investor, it causes him to fall deeply and hopelessly in love with a stock under false pretenses. The misleading insider information makes a given investment seem far more attractive than it really is, and his lust is such that he can't wait to put his money down.

For the wrathful investor, insider tips get him coming and going. He is so angry from past investing failures that when he receives inside information, he accepts it with a vengeance, feeling it's about time he had a little luck. Then, when he realizes the information was misleading and he starts losing money, he overreacts and sells his investment at a loss, failing to display the patience the situation might call for.

For the vain investor, inside information is a way to stroke his ego, to make him feel better than others. He is flattered that it was passed on to him, and he accepts it without question; it confirms his sense of privilege. When the information doesn't lead to a big win, though, he is slow to realize that the information was worthless; his pride prevents him from making this admission quickly.

For the investing glutton, this is an opportunity to invest with abandon. The inside info he thinks he possesses gives him a chance to get in on the action, to experience the thrill of making fast, significant buys. No doubt, an investing glutton can feast for days on the tip he received from his broker, barber, or cab driver.

I realize this last sentence was a bit flip, but I remain amazed at how people get suckered into buying and selling mistakes based on alleged insider information. To help you avoid allowing your sins to get the better of you, start out by recognizing the following facts about insider information.

IT'S ILLEGAL!

You would think this would be obvious, but when investors are in the grip of their sins, they often rationalize away the illegality. They tell themselves that insider trading is only something big shots get convicted for, that if their barber passes on a piece of information to them, it's really not insider trading because their barber isn't an insider. The Securities Exchange Commission, however, won't agree with this rationalization. If you actually happen to come across real inside stuff and act upon it, you can be caught, prosecuted, and convicted faster than you can say "Martha Stewart." The SEC has the power to subpoena all trading records, telephone calls, and anything else that might prove their case against you.

IT'S ILLUSORY

I suppose the good news is that you are unlikely to be convicted of insider trading because the information you receive is probably worthless. The bad news is that you'll lose money. In the overwhelming majority of cases, inside information is nothing more than gossip and guesses. Many times, it reaches your ears after it has been filtered through multiple sources—your brother-in-law's neighbor works for an ad agency whose client told him such and such. Sometimes, unethical brokers and other investing professionals start false rumors for their own purposes. Even when there is some accuracy to the information you receive, you probably are receiving it a day late and a dollar short. By the time you know about it, so do thousands of others, and you have missed your window to take advantage of it.

To prevent yourself from yielding to whatever sin you're most vulnerable to, ask yourself the following questions when you find yourself in insider information situations:

Have I done any due diligence on the company in question?

Have I gone over the company's financial statements and earnings estimates?

If I were to eliminate the one piece of information that makes me excited about this stock, is there anything else about the company that would make me think it would be a good investment?

How much of this information that I've received has already been priced into the stock?

In real-life situations, of course, it is sometimes difficult to ask these questions before acting. Here is a cautionary tale to keep in mind the next time you're privy to what sounds like inside information.

Jack read an article in a prominent business publication mentioning a number of retail companies that might be possible takeover targets in the next few years, and one of them was Dillard's, a department store chain based in the South. A week later, he was at a party and he happened to overhear a conversation in which someone who worked for a competing department store mentioned that Dillard's was bound to be bought within the year. Jack is convinced he knows something very few others do, and because avarice is a sin to which he is particularly vulnerable, a voice inside his head is crying out for him to make this investment, telling him he's a coward and a fool if he hesitates.

Another, more rational voice, though, suggests he do a little research before making the plunge. It takes Jack all of two minutes to learn that Dillard's is trading at a price-to-earnings ratio of 20 and the rest of the industry is at 15, suggesting that a takeover may have already been priced into the stock.

Panic Situations

The market or a particular sector in which you're heavily invested experiences a downturn. You have taken a strong position in a company that is the subject of a headline-making governmental investigation. You have just made an investment in a fund that has gone up for ten straight quarters, and you receive the bad news that for the first time in almost three years, it went down. These are potential panic situations, and while your impulse to act quickly may be correct, it may also end up being a rash action. If you are vulnerable to sins such as sloth, anger, and gluttony, you are likely to act rashly.

Slothful investors are particularly vulnerable to these situations because they often are passive investors, keeping track of their investments sporadically at best. When they finally look at their brokerage statement and realize their portfolio has lost 10 percent of its value, they are likely to overreact. Rather than analyzing the reasons for the decline and considering whether it is more prudent to wait out the situation, they sell as fast as they can, rousing themselves from their lethargy at exactly the wrong time.

Angry investors, on the other hand, tend to react to panic situations with a fury that clouds their judgment. They ask questions that are ultimately irrelevant to their investing decisions: "How could the CEO have let the situation deteriorate to this point? Why didn't my broker anticipate the government investigation and warn me about it?" They are so angry that all they can do is look backwards and second guess rather than gather information in order to move forward. The questions investors should ask in these situations include:

Has the fundamental situation for the stock changed?

Will earnings be affected for the long term?

Is there legal action that may impair the company?

Is my holding too large relative to my net worth?

If I were to sell in reaction to my panicky feeling, is the price acceptable or will I suffer a serious loss?

Am I becoming anxious because I suddenly learned of this negative situation? If I had been following its development for weeks or months instead of days, would I be reacting so emotionally to what is taking place?

To help you understand how to prevent your sinful tendencies from surfacing in panic scenarios, let's walk through a typical one.

On October 14, 2004, the New York attorney general's office announced that it was charging insurance broker Marsh & McLennan (MMC) with taking excessive commissions from their clients. The stock

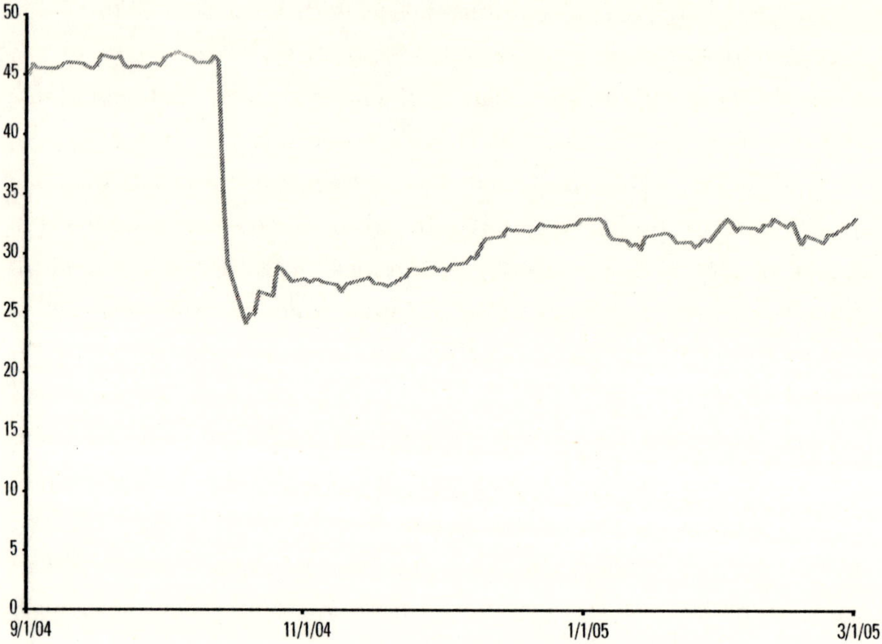

Marsh & McLennan: 9/1/2004–3/1/2005

had been trading around $45 per share for the previous few months, and this news caused it to drop to $35 immediately. It seemed to settle in at this price for a few days, and then began drifting higher. More bad news about Marsh & McLennan's commissions emerged, however, sending the price down to around $25–$28 a share.

For the slothful investor who didn't realize what was happening until he opened his October statement and saw his holding was now worth $27.66 per share, the desire to sell would be overwhelming. Rather than wait for the fundamentally solid stock to head back into positive territory, he would have sold in that exquisitely painful moment of panic. On the other hand, a lustful investor would have probably been caught in the switches. In other words, when his beloved Marsh & McLennan stock tumbled on the bad news, he probably would have refused to sell. But when it started to come back, he undoubtedly would have bought more and then been burned twice when the second wave of bad news hit.

To get through panic situations such as this one, recognize the typical bad news scenario and how it impacts a given stock. In most instances when a stock price drops suddenly because of a negative event, the stock finds a price quickly where fresh investor money is attracted to it. People who are looking for a bounce after the bad news drop or those who believe it is oversold start buying, and the stock consolidates around the new price. If there is no further bad news or some of the early negative media stories are followed up by positive or "corrective" ones (that suggest the earlier, negative reports were exaggerated), the stock price often drifts higher. This prompts additional buying. Many times, new revelations about misconduct, fraud, economic woes, and so on emerge and send the stock price even lower than its earlier low point (because in most cases, where there's smoke, there's fire).

Being aware of this typical scenario can help you look at events objectively rather than sliding into an emotional selling or buying reaction based on your sin vulnerabilities.

No matter what your particular vulnerabilities might be, the best preventative advice I can offer is: Keep your portfolio diversified and don't allow any individual stock holding to exceed 3 percent of your net worth. As an investor, you need to be prepared for negative events that will cause you to lose your cool. It has happened to me—I was holding Merck and Mirant Energy at the wrong times—and it makes your palms start to sweat. You are able to take a step back from this extremely anxious posture if you're sufficiently diversified, though, and rethink whatever action your panic was causing you to contemplate.

Disappointing Returns

Most obviously, investing gluttons and those especially vulnerable to greed and envy find themselves reacting irrationally when performance dips. Sometimes it takes little more than a small decline reflected in their monthly statements to trigger this response. Other times, they require more substantial declines. In either instance, though, they act rashly and prematurely. They switch advisors or funds or sell stocks because they overreact to declines. Certainly investment performance must be monitored and changes made if a stock is in free fall or if an advisor is incompetent, but the point here is that certain situations cause investors to react sinfully rather than with common sense.

For instance, greedy investors continuously "chase performance," responding poorly to situations that cause them to lose ground in this chase. For instance, during a year when the S&P 500 rose 9 percent, an investor's portfolio rose 10.5 percent. This greedy and envious investor, however, fired his advisor because he had a friend whose advisor specialized in small cap stocks and his portfolio increased 18 percent during this same time period. This reaction may seem ludicrous when reading about it, but for this particular investor, it made perfect sense. His envy offered him clear evidence that his friend's advisor had done a better job than his had done; his greed drove him to lick his chops at the prospect of making all the money his friend had made. He switched without considering that his current advisor had helped him create a balanced portfolio that would help him achieve his long-term goals and that would not subject him to the same risks as if he were heavily invested in small caps.

Perhaps less obviously, some greedy and envious investors are so vulnerable to their sins that they bend over backwards to avoid any potentially underperforming investment. They only want to purchase the hottest stocks and funds or to work with the top fund managers and advisors. They want others to envy the professionals they have chosen to advise them, and they want to rake in the money that choosing exactly the right investments all the time will yield. Of course, this is nonsense, but it makes perfect sense when you are myopically focused on winners. I've referred earlier to the peril of jumping on bandwagons too late, especially the way people climbed on board technology stocks in the late 1990s and watched them plummet. In 2006, people are flocking to Real Estate Investment Trusts (REITs), a sector that has risen over 135 percent in the last six years including dividends. Yields from REITs, though, are only about half as much as they were six years ago. Where were these same investors when REITs were out of favor and the stocks were 50 percent lower?

Vanguard REIT Index: 1/1/1999–9/1/2005

Gluttons are especially likely to respond poorly to negative performance. They are always looking for an excuse to make an investment change, and they are likely to overreact to declines that wouldn't bother other investors. It is almost as if they believe they can keep ahead of the game by switching investments or advisors before everyone else. As a result, they often miss the upside of a stock or fund and experience primarily the downside.

We should also note that disappointing returns create a situation that can negatively influence other sinful investors. The lust-driven investor, for instance, tends to underreact to poor performance. Unlike the other sins, this one causes people to rationalize their losses and fail to identify an advisor who is doing a bad job or a stock or fund that needs to be dumped. They are so enamored of a particular investor's past performance or reputation that they refuse to believe the negative evidence in front of their eyes. Sloth, too, can contribute to inaction when any logical, objective investor would take action. Moving money from one advisor to another may require a confrontation or at least raise the possibility of conflict, something slothful investors seek to avoid—it takes a lot of energy to confront someone. In addition, moving investments to a new advisor demands times and effort—finding the new advisor, filling out paperwork, and so on.

I have a good friend who has placed his $3 million portfolio with an investment advisor who was his college roommate. He shared with me that the performance over a three-year period was mediocre, but that he was reluctant to move the money because of friendship with the advisor. Given that this advisor is underperforming at about 2 percent per annum, the loss over a ten-year period would be around $657,000 compared to if the money were with an "average" advisor.

If you find that your particular sins cause you to overreact or underreact to disappointing news, try doing the following:

USE AN APPROPRIATE BENCHMARK TO MEASURE WHETHER A DISAPPOINTING PERFORMANCE JUSTIFIES MAKING A CHANGE

Use a blend of the S&P 500 and a broad bond market index like the Lehman aggregate. If you are a somewhat more aggressive investor, incorporate the Russell 2000 or NASDAQ. Compare your performance to the benchmark annually, and only then determine whether a change is justified. If your investments are performing significantly below the norm, then a change may be called for. If this poor performance represents a pattern—it has been similarly disappointing for two or more years in a row—then there is even more reason to consider a change.

USE A THREE-YEAR BENCHMARK TO MEASURE PERFORMANCE IF YOUR QUARTERLY OR ANNUAL RESULTS ARE IN THE GRAY AREA BETWEEN AVERAGE AND A BIT BELOW AVERAGE

This is a good horizon for most investors, providing sufficient time to give stocks, funds, or advisors a chance to prove their worth. Although a big dip in performance may call for more immediate action, your patience will be rewarded if you have made wise choices in the beginning. Recognize that your greed, envy, and gluttony may cause you to jump the gun, and frequent switching of investments and advisors is usually a bad idea. Similarly, be aware that sloth and lust may cause you to rationalize poor performance, and three years is the outside limit to tolerate disappointing returns.

UNDERSTAND YOUR FUND CATEGORY AND COMPARE IT WITH SIMILAR CATEGORY FUNDS

Investors are fond of comparing apples and oranges, and their reactions to what seems like poor performance may actually be the result of a bad comparison or a misunderstanding of their fund. Let us say you invest in the Longleaf Partners (LLPFX) Mutual Fund. As a fund in the large capitalization value stock category, it may not rise as quickly as a growth fund in a "hot" market. What you're getting with this fund is stability in a falling market, and if you expect it to perform like a growth fund, you're bound to be disappointed. Therefore, compare your performance with other similar funds that can be found listed in *Barron's*, the *Wall Street Journal*, and Yahoo! Finance. If your fund is consistently in the lower half of performance compared to competitors, look for a new fund.

Schemes and Strategies: Can't-Miss Approaches That Often Do

At some point during their investing, people discover a technique or investment strategy that seems too good to be true. They attend a seminar that teaches strategies guaranteed to produce great wealth. They read a book that convinces them that a nondollar currency investment is a foolproof approach to obtain superior returns. They see a late-night infomercial that makes a credible case for penny stocks. They read a newsletter that describes a highly sophisticated, mathematically-based charting technique and know that once they master it, they will be able to use it to make money in the market.

Though you may have detected a note of skepticism in my descriptions of these techniques, other people find them totally credible. In fact, they may possess some validity for some people when used expertly and judiciously. At times, the seminars and newsletter descriptions are sophisticated and convincing, and people looking for a "magical" approach to investing will surely find one.

These situations, however, are tailor-made for sinful investors. The prospect of a sure-fire strategy brings out our greed, lust, and all the other sins. To help you understand how this is so, let's focus on a strategy that has some validity and has taken the investing world by storm, but that usually triggers each of the seven sins, often leading to disastrous results.

Hedge funds are loosely regulated partnerships that can invest in almost anything that can generate a positive return. Some hedge fund tactics include capitalizing on yield differentials between different currencies or finding stocks to buy against selling a similar, potentially overvalued stock. As a hedge fund investor, your money is commingled with others, and you may not even know what securities the fund holds. Perhaps most significantly, the hedge fund manager takes a large percentage of any returns, including around 20 percent of any profits plus a 1 to 2 percent management fee. When funds are pooled together in "funds of funds," management fees can be 3 percent plus 30 percent of profits. The reason for this increase is that investors have "experts" picking the hedge funds for them and they receive instant diversification. What most people don't realize is that if the funds produce a 12 percent gross return, they will only end up with 6.3 percent before taxes. Since most of these gains are short-term so the net after-tax return will be around 4 percent, not much better than a municipal bond.

Hedge funds are also subject to fraud. In the fall of 2005, for instance, the hedge fund run by Bayou Management shut down and left investors with significant losses. Highly publicized returns of close to 40 percent in the late 1990s attracted $500 million to the fund, and it may be that at one point, the fund was performing as spectacularly as publicized. Eventually, though, the returns dropped, and fraud was committed, perhaps in response to intense pressure to maintain those spectacular returns. I'm not suggesting that you should avoid hedge funds because of the possibility of fraud, but because they create situations where the seven sins flourish. Hedge funds became increasingly attractive after the tech bubble burst and the major stock averages collapsed. In 2000 when the S&P 500 dropped 10 percent and the NASDAQ lost over 39 percent, many hedge funds posted returns over 10 percent. It should come as no surprise that over $1 trillion is invested in these funds.

Most hedge funds today are competing against each other for an ever-diminishing return. At times, they take a higher degree of risk than in the past to capitalize on small market opportunities. While some funds have a history of solid returns and excellent management and may have a place in a high-net-worth investor's portfolio, I would urge the average investor (under $500,000 net worth) to avoid them because whatever sin vulnerability you have, it will come out in the hedge fund investing process. Specifically, here are the sins and how to counteract their effects:

Envy

People are usually drawn to all magical techniques and strategies because they heard about someone else who made a killing using a particular form of magic. They are envious beyond belief, especially if they feel that their investments are producing average results at best. You can well imagine the envy of someone in 2000 who was heavily invested in stocks and heard about someone who was getting a 10 percent return from a hedge fund investment.

If you find yourself envying investors in hedge funds or any "can't miss" vehicle, do an experiment. Use one of the Internet sites that allow you to track average hedge fund returns. One site that is reliable is cisdm.som.umass.edu. Select the type of hedge fun you were considering from the vast array of investment styles and pretend you're investing a sizable amount of money in a hedge fund. Track its performance over an extended period of time after deducting 40% for taxes and see if you're still envious.

Greed

The prospect of 35 or 40 percent returns is enough to make even a saint greedy. Counteract this greed by: 1) Reminding yourself that of the 8,000 hedge funds, only a tiny percentage provide this incredible return.

2) Asking a financial advisor to tell you the net after-tax average return for the past year of hedge funds he handles or knows about. 3) Telling yourself that you're investing for the long haul, and that the stock market's average return of over 11 percent for the last eighty years will help you meet most long-term goals.

Gluttony

Hedge funds and other higher risk vehicles cause investing gluttons to place too much of their portfolio in them. In the glutton's mind, this incredible opportunity mandates against nibbling. It is time to go whole hog, and so an investor places far more money in a hedge fund than he should.

To stop yourself from making this mistake, force yourself to limit the money you put into nontraditional investments to less than 20 percent of your net worth and no more than 5 percent in any single fund. If you've been seduced by hedge funds, remind yourself that while fraud is just a slight possibility, it should give you pause. Also, in years when equity markets perform well, you are likely to receive lower returns in a hedge fund.

Sloth

People frequently fail to look beyond the initial, highly positive numbers when they hear about a great investment strategy. They content themselves with whatever partial information they have and don't do their homework to find out the whole story.

To overcome the effects of laziness when it comes to hedge funds, review audited financial statements from the funds. Talk to other investors with experience in this area. Investigate whether the hedge fund manager has a record of previous securities violations. All this represents relatively little work to prevent a relatively large loss.

Lust

One of the big dangers of these highly attractive investment opportunities is that people don't want to disabuse themselves of their fantasies.

They love to fall in love with hedge funds and other, seemingly brilliant investment strategies.

Here, the advice is simple: Force yourself to take a step back from your obsession with a given vehicle and create a written analysis of its pros and cons. Putting the facts on paper can jolt you out of your obsessed stupor. It also helps to have an investment advisor you trust give you an objective analysis of whatever fund or approach you think you're in love with.

Pride

After people experience the high of discovering what they feel is a great investment and boasting about it to others, they find it difficult to swallow their pride and get out when the signs point them toward an exit. Big losses occur over time, and if you're too stubborn to admit you made a mistake, you're likely to incur these losses.

Swallowing your pride is difficult, especially after you've congratulated yourself on finding the perfect investment approach, but it's the only way you won't throw good money after bad. The best thing to do in these circumstances is scare yourself silly. As you start losing money, do a calculation about how much money you might lose if the investment continues its current performance over the next year.

Anger

Anger tends to rear its ugly head late in the game. At some point, an investor must face reality and accept that he has committed a sin, and a dumb one at that. He asks himself how he could have been so naïve? He shakes his fist at the heavens and vows never to make this same mistake again. As a result, he not only avoids all investment approaches with a significant amount of risk, but parks his money in the most conservative vehicles he can find, earning a pittance on his investment.

The commonsense alternative is to adopt a long-term, highly diversified strategy that errs on the side of caution. In this way, you can still take advantage of the market's long-term upward trend and feel comfortable that your downside risk is relatively small.

Trick or Trend: Knowing When to Ride the Wave, When to Jump Off, and When to Keep Away in the First Place

Trends happen, and those who spot them as they're just emerging, ride them well and get off at precisely the right time make a great deal of money. As I've indicated, this is a very difficult thing to do. Unless you're a professional observer of the markets with outstanding insights and great powers of observation, you'll likely come upon the trend too late. The problem: It doesn't seem too late. You're bombarded with news stories about the rise of energy stocks or how blue chips are back or how the cell phone industry is about to introduce a new technology that will create huge profits in the industry. Because of the Internet and multimedia communication devices, these trends are dramatized to the point that we feel we should be taking advantage of them, and that if we're not, we're missing the boat. I have documented in a number of chapters how the tech mania that swept the country devastated portfolios of people who didn't see that the bubble was going to burst. When you're in the midst of a buying frenzy and every day the media documents how much tech stocks have risen, it's very difficult to gain perspective and see that the trend has crested and a major correction is imminent.

Envious and lustful investors are especially vulnerable to trends, as are those suffering from excess pride or gluttony. The envious see others making money because of a trend and get swept up in the excitement, failing to ask the questions that will help them determine if they're too late to benefit or if they should at least exercise caution; their envy robs them of their patience. Lustful investors fall in love with the idea of being part of the trend—they believe biotechs can do no wrong or that the Asian market is as beautiful an opportunity as they've ever encountered. Their lust causes them to lose all objectivity, and they fail to compare and contrast the object of their affection with other prospective investments. Proud investors are so eager to boast that they too are invested in a given, hot sector that they move much too quickly, eager to be the first on their block to say they've taken a major position in the sector (though often, they are far from being the first). Gluttons unbalance their portfolios because of hot trends, buying too much because the trend makes certain investments so appealing.

Don't let trends make you move too fast, buy too much, or fail to ask the right questions. That's easy to write, of course, but in the frenzy that often accompanies trends, it can be difficult to put these instructions into practice. Therefore, here is some more practical advice:

CREATE A TREND TIMELINE

Do some online research, finding when the trend was first reported on in periodicals or elsewhere (Web sites, broadcast outlets, newsletters). Was the most recent mention within the past week? Within the past month? Within the past year? Ideally, you'll invest based on the trend before it even hits the media. Realistically, you might be okay if you do so within days or weeks of its being reported. Any later, though, and you're in danger of investing as the trend's benefits quickly diminish.

PREDICT WHEN THE BUBBLE WILL BURST

Clearly, this is an extremely difficult prediction to make. However, history does tend to repeat itself in the financial markets and the more knowledge you can gain, the better prepared you will be. What you can do is chart earlier trends and determine how long they lasted and how suddenly they went from hot trend to yesterday's news. Focus on how trends unfolded in Biotech, Telecom, Utilities, and Semiconductors. A little research will reveal that the great investment opportunities existed primarily when the trend emerged and that the end was sudden and caught most people by surprise.

These two steps should help you approach trend investments cautiously and with the end in sight.

Situational Alerts

You can probably predict which situations are going to catalyze your sinful behaviors if you think back to how you behaved in similar investing situations in the past. If you have been investing for any period of time, it's likely that you found yourself in all four situation categories we've described. You may not remember, however, how these situations influenced your investment decision-making without a little help. To jog your memory, I've created the following questions related to each of the situations. As you answer the following multiple choice questions, you should be able to find at least one situation type that made you sin in the past and will likely do so in the future unless you're vigilant against it:

INSIDE INFORMATION

1. When I received a hot tip from a friend or colleague about a stock, I:

A. Dismissed the information as an unsubstantiated rumor.

B. Took the tip seriously and did a significant amount of research to determine its veracity.

C. Made a small investment based on the tip but did not do much research.

D. Invested a bundle immediately on the assumption that this was a chance of a lifetime to make a mint.

PANIC SITUATIONS

2. When I saw that a company or sector in which I was heavily invested was in serious trouble, I:

A. Gave myself time to consider my options, do my homework, and see how the situation played out before I made a decision.

B. Sold off some of my stake in the stock or sector after a little while but forced myself to be calm and objective as I monitored the market so I could determine the next best move.

C. Tried being patient for a day or two but found myself so anxiety-ridden that I had to sell the majority of my stake before it was too late.

D. Sold everything immediately.

DISAPPOINTING RETURNS

3. When I received my annual statement and found that the performance of my investments was below my expectations, I:

   A. Examined the context for the less-than-optimum performance, talked to my advisor, made comparisons with similar investments, and then made my decision.

   B. Became angry at the relatively poor performance and made some small but significant changes after some analysis.

   C. Made some changes to certain aspects of my portfolio; didn't compare investments but looked at what lost the most and got rid of those poor performers.

   D. Made major changes; found a new advisor; completely switched my investing strategy.

SCHEMES AND STRATEGIES

4. When I heard about hedge funds and their superior performance in this market, I:

   A. Talked to my advisor and did some investigation on my own about these funds and decided that now was not a good time to put my money in them.

   B. Placed a small percentage of my total assets in one fund that my advisor recommended.

   C. Placed a moderate amount of money in a fund that I read about on the Internet and that a number of a Web site's experts recommended.

   D. Found a hedge fund that all the investing pundits said returned the highest amount of any fund in the past year and put a significant amount of my assets into it.

TRICK OR TREND

5. When I discovered a market trend and saw the excitement building around it, I:

   A. Analyzed the trend thoroughly, determining when it started and when it was likely to end by doing research and consulting with financial advisors.

   B. Acted quickly to take advantage of the trend so I didn't do as much research as I should have, but I limited my investment to keep my portfolio diversified.

   C. Waited until I was sure the trend was for real and then when it was clear everyone and his brother were making similar investments, I took the plunge.

   D. As soon as I read about this trend in *Time* magazine (where it was featured on the cover) I shifted the majority of my portfolio into this sector, knowing that the early adopters were the ones who would reap the greatest benefits.

Clearly, the A answers indicate the least likelihood of sinning in a given situation and D answers represent the highest likelihood. While all investors given the right set of circumstances can commit a sin in any situation, the past is prologue, as Shakespeare once said. Most of you will find that one of these five situations elicited a D response, and this is the situation for which you must be on high alert.

10

We Are All Sinners, but Some of Us Can Be Saved

While working on this book, I have mentioned its premise to friends, and they have asked if it's really possible for people to change. Specifically, they wonder if bad or average investors can become good ones, if someone whose investing is driven by anger or envy can develop a level-headed, long-term mindset.

My answer is always an unequivocal "Yes." My response is based not only on my observation of investors who have followed a sin-free investing approach but on my belief that people can make dramatic changes in their lives if they put their minds to it and possess a simple but effective plan for change. Just as some people try to lose weight through faddish diets and fail, others use Weight Watchers or some other easy-to-follow diet plan, persevere and reach their goals.

One of the things I like best about the Seven Sins methodology is that it's easy to use. It doesn't involve complex formulas or require you to acquire volumes of new knowledge. It simply asks that you be aware of the seven sins, think about which ones in particular apply to you and make use of the ideas and tools to manage your sinful tendencies. If you do this regularly, you stand a good chance of dramatically improving your investing.

Many people don't believe this is possible, however, because they have read books and attended seminars that promised them the moon, and they discovered that when they put these methods into action, they didn't work.

I'm not promising you the moon. What I am promising is that you can change from a losing or mediocre short-term investor into a good long-term one. This may not seem as exciting as becoming an instant millionaire through an esoteric strategy, but it is tremendously rewarding to reach ambitious goals over time, and that's what this book is designed to help you do.

With this goal in mind, I'd like to spend this final chapter providing you with additional tools to help you manage the seven sins (and three additional, related sins), including "The Ten Commandments of Sin-Free Investing." I'll also discuss why in the coming months and years, people will be more vulnerable to their sinful tendencies than ever before. First, though, I would like to deliver a sermon of sorts, one designed to keep you from falling back into old habits.

Be Prepared to Be Shocked . . . or Change

Some of you may have picked up this book because of some shock to your investing system. You were going along fine for a while, but some event caused you to lose a lot of money in the market and you vowed to make a change. Others may have heard about a friend or colleague who suffered a major loss, and you want to prevent the same thing from happening to you. Without experiencing these shocks or seeing how they affect someone you know, it's easy to continue investing based on strong emotional states. If you haven't suffered a shock yet, you are bound to experience one if you lack a disciplined, long-term strategy.

In this last chapter, therefore, I would like to offer my fire and brimstone sermon about what happens to investors who ignore the sins to which they are most vulnerable. This is a cautionary sermon, one that I hope will keep you on a righteous investing path.

When I use the word shock, I am referring to how people reacted right after the NASDAQ reached 5,000 in March, 2000. In the two or three years before that, people who followed the seven sins approach would have made much less than high-tech gluttons and envy-driven investors. After that, though, they paid for their sins. When the market corrected and the NASDAQ lost 65 percent of its value during the next thirteen months, many investors were in shock. I know of professional, upper-middle-class people who found they couldn't afford to send their children to college or who realized that they would have to postpone their retirements for five or ten years. Even worse, the really sinful investors who took out margin loans to buy more stock went bankrupt or came close to it. It was no coincidence that after experiencing these calamitous losses, a growing number of people asked me about alternative, disciplined approaches to investing.

The shock is not always as all-encompassing as the NASDAQ's plunge. Sometimes, it can be related to one specific stock or company. For instance, an airline employee may have spent her entire career at Delta and took great pride in her company. Most of her portfolio consisted of Delta stock. She never diversified her holdings in large part because she thought the world of Delta and felt it would be disloyal to sell some of her Delta stock. Though her loyalty may have been admirable, her investing sin of pride did her in when the company went bankrupt and rendered her stock worthless.

Greed, too, sets up investors for shocks. In the world of real estate investing, for instance, the housing market goes through periods of phenomenal multiyear appreciation, inducing people to get in over their head. Even conservative investors can become caught up in what appears to be an endlessly rising market. One person decides to make money by "flipping" condos in Florida, becoming increasing bold as his profits grow. Another person buys a new and larger house and holds off selling the old house, since prices seem as if they will continue to climb. When the bottom falls out, they're stunned. Their greed caused them to ignore logic and believe that prices would rise far into the future.

Similarly, greed combined with lust often delivers shocks of the type Jack received. He thought WorldCom was a golden stock, and placed 90 percent of his net worth in it. Jack wasn't stupid; he knew that it was not always going to be a high flyer. His lust and greed, though, caused him to minimize the downside risk. He told himself that investing in WorldCom was like putting the majority of his money into Home Depot or Proctor & Gamble. He loved WorldCom so much and was so greedy for the high returns it produced that he wasn't assessing the company objectively, and so he threw caution and much of his life savings to the wind. It really was a shock to Jack when WorldCom went to the eighth circle of Dante's hell.

Consider, too, the shock received by my colleague, Don, who was buying and selling tech stocks just about every day. During this hot bubble market, Don did very well, even though he was committing at least five of the seven deadly sins. Though Don was a financial services professional, his sins caused him to fall into the amateur's trap of being sure that he would know when it was time to get out. No one knows when it's time to get out, especially when they are vain and greedy and have convinced themselves that every drop will be followed by a rebound. During this bubble market, Don would experience days when his portfolio would increase by as much as $20,000, so naturally he invested fast and furiously. He would even plunk down money on a stock despite knowing little about it, acting only on the recommendations of friends. He spent lavishly and boasted to everyone how he had the system beat.

When everything went south, Don lost over half his net worth and his portfolio was worth less than it was when the bull market started three years prior. It was a shock for him to realize not only that he had made foolish investing mistakes, but that his plans for retirement and other long-term goals had gone up in smoke.

The good news is, Don changed. He responded to the shock by vowing to invest in a more conservative, disciplined, long-term manner. He interviewed four investment advisors to help him achieve this goal and chose the one with whom he connected. Don would meet with his advisor twice each year and review his holdings and performance, resisting the urge to go back to his daily investing practices. As much as Don hated the experience he went through, he realized that it provided him with an epiphany: His investing philosophy was so warped by greed, envy, pride, lust, and gluttony that he would have lost all his money sooner or later. The shock of this epiphany helped him change how he invested.

Pat also experienced a change-inducing shock. A dentist who was successfully trading small-cap healthcare stocks, Pat managed his own portfolio as well as the portfolios of a few friends. At one point, he increased the value of these portfolios by 85 percent. His success, though, made him slothful, and he sometimes doubled down because the price dropped, and he didn't consider if fundamental or technical factors justified this strategy. He was also extremely proud of his small-cap healthcare approach and refused to believe that it was flawed in any way. When small-caps hit a rough period, though, Pat became well aware of the flaw as all the portfolios he managed lost a considerable amount of money.

Unlike Don, Pat responded more slowly to his expectations being thwarted. He went through a period of disbelief, anger, and sadness about all the money he had lost. It's fair to say that he went through a grieving process of sorts. During this time, he persisted with his small cap strategy, but he also began speaking to investment experts and reading articles that helped him realize he should try a more diversified approach. He eventually did some research and found a low-cost family of mutual funds, paying no load or sales charges. To date, his portfolio had grown steadily if not spectacularly, and Pat is diligent about adding a reasonable amount of money to these funds monthly.

The moral of these stories is that shock can be a catalyst for positive investing change. If I were delivering these stories as a sermon, however, I would shake my fist, raise my voice, and warn of the perils of two sins in particular and how they can prevent people from heeding the lessons of major losses.

Sloth and Pride: How They Prevent Investors from Responding Positively to Shock

Some investors experience significant losses but take counterproductive actions in the wake of these losses. Rather than becoming aware of how their sins created their investing woes, they allow sloth and pride to cloud their vision, shielding them from the truth about the mistakes they have made.

First, their pride causes them to become defensive about tactical errors or mistakes in strategy. When they suffer grievous losses, they respond by rationalizing, protesting, and scapegoating. Their pride convinces them that it could not possibly have been anything they did that caused their shocking losses, but that they were victimized by "market factors" or some other external event. It's likely that vanity was a sin they suffered from throughout their investing careers, but it comes on full steam after a major reversal of fortune. If they cannot get past their pride, they will continue making the same investing mistakes or even worse ones.

Second, I see a great deal of "slothful denial" in some investors when the bottom falls out. In other words, they use apathy, false hope, and fatalism to shield themselves from reality. Some may take a break from trading after misfortune befalls them or they may stop looking at their statements in order to deny that a situation is as bad as it is. They also delude themselves by insisting that their investments will recover from their losses or that some unlikely event will occur that will have them doing well in no time. Rather than doing the work necessary to assess the damage and figure out an alternative course of action, they seek refuge in inaction and ignorance.

If you have suffered a shocking downturn, you need to be vigilant against these two sins or you can become locked in this downward spiral and your bad investment situation can become worse. After a major setback, therefore, ask yourself the following questions:

Pride

When I suffered this major loss, did I immediately start looking for someone or something to blame?

Have I avoided analyzing my role in the loss; have I thought about whether my particular strategy was ruled more by emotion than by logic?

Until I suffered the loss, was I verbally proud of my investing approach; did I frequently talk about how it was ingenious, foolproof, and so on?

Is it possible that I don't want to face the fact that my investing approach was flawed and that by continuing to insist it was sound, I'm preserving my pride and endangering my pocketbook?

Sloth

After the major downturn in my investments, did I find that I was uninterested in the markets and stopped reading all the newsletters and visiting the online sites that formerly was part of my routine?

Did my investing become "sloppier" after a major setback; was I less interested in researching investments and monitoring specific companies and sectors?

Did I refuse to face the reality of my losses; did I make an effort to avoid the statements that charted the losses as they mounted?

Have I avoided making any changes in my strategy because I've convinced myself that doing so is premature and that the strategy is still viable; can I make a logical argument for this belief or is it more of a hunch?

Three Subtle Sins

Now that you've been forewarned about how pride and sloth can prevent you from heeding the red flags of major losses, you should also be on the lookout for three less obvious sins that fall just outside of the Biblical seven but are related to them. I've talked a little about each of them within the context of the other sins, but I want to give you a little more information about them so that they don't slip beneath your radar:

TEMPORARY EGOMANIA

This is a variation on our vanity theme, but it is more subtle because it is not an integral part of your investing approach; temporary egomania tends to erupt only in response to a certain type of situation. For instance, you find yourself on a roll and are convinced you've hit on exactly the right theory or strategy to make a bundle. Maybe you're making money in a market where everyone else seem to be losing or you've created what seems like an ingenious approach to minimize risk and maximize reward. Your ego, which is usually under control, shoots to the sky, and this inflated sense of self-worth causes you to put more money into the market than you normally would or to ignore your traditional diversified approach.

Many investors, at some point, will hit a hot streak. This is the time when they need to remind themselves that though their acumen may have helped them get on that streak, they are fallible. Whenever people start thinking they can outsmart the market, that's the moment when they start sowing the seeds of their own destruction. The antidote for temporary egomania, therefore, is simple: Whenever you hit a hot streak, be conscious that it is making you believe you can do no wrong, and this is exactly the time when you're likely to make a major investing mistake.

MULE-HEADEDNESS

Stubborn investors get stuck in ruts. Their sin is really a lack of flexibility. While they may have the knowledge and skills to be good investors, their inability to adjust to changing situations causes them to lose money. For example, an investor who made money in drug stocks in the 1990s refuses to consider other sectors because of his success in this one sector. Going against the facts, he insists to himself and others that the sector is going to rebound. Mule-headedness is a variation on the sin of lust because of the insistence on sticking with one particular sector, stock, fund, or method, but it may not involve a conscious, emotional attachment. Sometimes, stubborn investors believe they are being objective and logical, though in reality they are unwilling to invest outside of their comfort zone. Their analysis is flawed because they have a fixed idea of what constitutes a good investment, and they don't let the facts get in the way of their flawed reasoning.

For instance, some investors that did well during the growth-oriented 1990s had great difficulty transitioning to the next decade of lower returns and yields. In the 1990s, many of them could have cared less about dividend rates, but in the current decade, these rates have a key effect on equity valuations and ultimately, returns. Stubbornly, however, they refuse to factor dividends into their investment decision-making and ignore companies with dividend yields near 4 percent that have a history of increasing this rate annually.

Consider, too, an older investor who has been investing for forty years. He has avoided all foreign investments because early in his investing career, it was difficult to make these investments. Plus, all the experts warned that most foreign investments were extremely risky. Today, though, hundreds of legitimate, conservative foreign funds exist. In fact, a Fidelity study in 2004 found that a portfolio with some non-U.S. exposure will generally have a higher return with lower volatility than one without this exposure. Stubbornness, however, prevents these individuals from absorbing these facts and adjusting their portfolio accordingly.

Here, the antidote is questioning your fixed investing patterns regularly. Recognize, too, that a difference exists between being confident and resolute and being so mule-headed that you refuse to consider any alternatives.

TIMIDITY

Some people are overly cautious by nature. Others become this way after the type of market shock I described earlier. In either case, they become such timid investors that they put all their money into CDs, money market accounts, or add a few token blue chip stocks or extremely conservative funds to the mix. A sure sign that you're guilty of timidity is if you can't tolerate seeing your investments go down in value. No one likes to see this happen, but if you really understand how the market works, you can tolerate these inevitable dips. Remind yourself that if you keep your money in CDs and money market accounts, over time, taxes and inflation will reduce your real return to zero. Remind yourself, too, that the equity market over the long run will compensate you for the risks you're taking and the decreases in value you must be able to tolerate over the short term. Obviously, you don't want to be foolish and take too many risks, but you do need to find a middle ground between a cash-under-the-mattress mentality and the Las Vegas mindset.

The Ten Commandments of Sin-Free Investing

To help you manage the three secondary sins just mentioned as well as the seven major ones, I've put together a list of ten things you should and should not do. They compliment the sins, in that they are action items as opposed to "warnings." Just as the ten commandments of biblical fame suggest ways to avoid the seven sins, these commandments function in a similar manner. Keeping a list of these commandments handy next to a list of the sins should provide you with the model you need to maintain your virtuous investment path. Let's look at each commandment and how to obey it:

Thou shall not covet thy neighbor's investments.

When your neighbor, friend, relative, or colleague makes a bundle through investing, remind yourself to manage the envy you naturally feel. If you don't manage this envy, you're likely to copy his strategy or type of investment. It's possible (though unlikely) that copying it may be effective in the short-term, but it is no way to meet long-term objectives. Viewed without any context or history, a buddy's great investment is not always what it appears. He may have been investing in food-related companies for years without much success, but he happened to be holding one food company stock that shot skyward because of some hugely successful product introduction. You are not privy to the years of futility as he pursued this approach; all you see is that a food company investment paid off handsomely. If you try and duplicate his "strategy," you're doing so without seeing the whole picture. If you possessed this broader perspective, you would never attempt to use his flawed approach.

Diminish your fervor to copy other successful tactics and techniques by asking your neighbor or colleague the following questions: How long have you had this particular investment? How has it done over the last three years? Have you ever had a similarly spectacular success in the past ten years? Have you been disappointed by your investing approach over the last five years? How were you disappointed? The answers are likely to make you less covetous.

Thou shall not make a killing.

Are you actively looking for the next Dell? Do you want to find a stock that is under $1 a share (as Dell was, split adjusted, prior to 1996) and ride it to $50 (which Dell reached in 2000)? If this is what your goal is, you are better off studying gambling techniques and visiting a casino. Trying to make a killing causes you to invest in stocks that carry a lot of risk and that have relatively low odds of rewarding the risks you take.

If you feel the urge to make a killing and you're particularly vulnerable to sins such as greed and gluttony, here is a good way to follow this commandment. Tell yourself that if you want to make a killing, rather than searching for a rags-to-riches stock, your money would be better spent by taking a risk on:

- Opening a restaurant
- Starting an Internet grocery store
- Buying real estate
- Buying swamp land in Zimbabwe

I'm not suggesting you actually do these things, only that you should consider them and then realize how much risk is involved in trying to make a killing in the market.

Know thy investments better than thou know thyself.

If you're an investing glutton or driven by lust, you're likely to act first and ask questions later. While certain situations may call for immediate investing action, most require contemplation and investigation before making a decision. At some point, you probably bought a stock without knowing all the metrics, such as price-to-earning ratio, price to sales, cash flow, and book value. You've probably also bought a mutual fund without being aware of all the fees involved. You may have been so anxious to purchase a stock on the upswing that you failed to learn much about the company, including who the CEO is, the company's products and services, its performance over the past year, and so on.

In almost all of these instances, you probably regretted your investment.

For long-term investors, slow is almost always better than fast. To remind yourself of this fact, consider the following scenario. You decide you want to buy the S&P 100 because you're convinced that it's going to do very well in the coming year. You're well aware that it has increased in value significantly in the last week, and you want to make the investment before it goes too much higher. Your investment advisor tells you about a fund with a good reputation, North Track S&P 100 Index Fund (SPPCX). The fund charges 1.88 percent annually or $188 per $10,000 invested. At first that rate sounds reasonable, and in your rush to invest, you may not investigate other funds and their charges. If this were the case, you might miss the S&P 100 Trust (OEF) that only charges .20 percent annually or $20 per $10,000 invested. If you assume the S&P 100 appreciates just 6 percent per annum, and you invest $10,000 per year, the difference in fees alone will amount to over $10,000 at the end of ten years.

Thou shall not make unto thee a graven image of profits.

In other words, don't worship profits and take them just because you have them. As tempting as it is to book a profit when stocks do well, many times it's wiser to hold on to the stock and wait for its price to rise further over time. Before making a decision, examine the company before you bought it, look at what has transpired since, and then ask yourself the following questions:

Have the earnings grown faster than market expectations?

Has there been some positive event that may allow for greater growth in the future?

Be aware, too, that if you have held the stock for months or even years without much positive movement and it suddenly shoots up, your temptation will be to sell in what seems an anomalous period. Before selling, though, do your research and see if this really is anomaly or if it is just the start of a longer-lasting upward trend.

I remember buying Cummins, Inc. (CMI), an Indiana-based engine manufacturer, at $32 in 2001. The company was experiencing a slowdown in sales and earnings were declining. The stock struggled, bottomed out at $20 and finally recovered to the upper $30s by the middle of 2004. Relieved that the stock had made a respectable comeback, I sold at $39 and made a modest profit. What I failed to do was track a clear change in the sales and profit momentum of the company. My avarice got the better of me. If I had waited until late 2006, I would have seen the stock climb to $100 as earnings were poised to exceed $10 per share for the year.

Thou shall not take the name of the Lord in vain or issue any foul-tempered oaths while investing.

This one is simple. Don't invest with vengeance in your heart or any heated emotion driving your decision-making. Wrath, envy, and vanity are three of the sins that can cause you to invest in highly emotional states. You need to be aware of your emotional temperature when considering an investment, and if you find yourself upset, thinking about getting revenge, or furious at friend, foe, or the investment vehicle itself, give yourself a time out for a day or longer. Calm investors have a far better track record than highly emotional ones, and you need to keep this in mind or you'll become even angrier when your hot-tempered investment doesn't pan out.

Thou shall not commit adultery chasing some flashy little stock of the moment.

As much as I repeat this commandment, I know that daily price movements seduce people into betraying their long-term commitments and go for the most attractive investment at that particular moment. To put it more bluntly: Don't buy something just because it's "hot." Once you recognize that it's hot, you're probably already too late. Force yourself to think long-term, even when you're tempted by what seems to be a short-term sure thing.

Honor thy mother, thy father, and the market in good times and bad.

This is a counterintuitive commandment. Normally, when the market experiences a significant downward trend, people sell off some of their holdings or even get out completely. Vanity makes it hard for people to face their portfolio's decline in value. Anger with the market makes them want to get out. Instead, these down periods are opportunities to invest a bit more than normal.

In moments of doubt, consider these facts: The Dow dipped below 8,000 after 9/11/01, but then rose to over 10,700 within six months. At the beginning of the Iraq war in March 2003, the Dow went below 7,400 and was over 10,000 by the end of the year.

The market is more resilient than anyone thinks during the times when it reaches its nadir. Time and again, it has bounced back, and you want to be invested in it when it springs upward.

Thou shall not steal from thyself by forgetting about taxes.

I am always amazed when investors fail to consider after-tax returns in assessing their performance. Perhaps this oversight is a direct result of the sin of pride—they can't puff up their feathers and crow as loudly with an after-tax return number. Perhaps it's a result of envy—they are driven to brag about their great results and lesser results won't allow them to respond effectively to their feelings of envy. Perhaps it's simply sloth—they are too lazy to think about the difference between after-tax returns and pre-tax returns or to do the math. Whatever sin causes them not to obey this commandment, they end up deluding themselves about how well their investments are doing.

Similarly, some investors sell a stock before it becomes eligible for capital gains treatment. For investors in the highest tax bracket, the difference is 15 percent instead of 35 percent if they hold the stock for a year and a day. Gluttons, of course, lack the patience to hold their stocks for that long. Angry investors, too, may be so upset that a stock has failed to meet their expectations that they may sell it because they have so much animosity toward it, heedless of the tax consequences.

If you want to adhere to this commandment, ask yourself the following questions:

Am I using every possible dollar in tax-deferred, retirement-type vehicles, such as IRAs or 401(k)s?

Am I taking full advantage of 529 college savings plans?

When thinking about fixed-income investing in a fully taxable account, am I aware of all my tax-exempt options and what the net yields are?

Thou shall not worship false idols or deceitful financial advisors.

Is your advisor or broker honest with you about his motivation and how he is compensated? Beware of brokers who try and sell you that their superior performance and low annual fees will more than compensate you for a 5 percent upfront charge. You should not pay a load or sales charge when buying a mutual fund, but people routinely do. Similarly, steer clear of advisors who use "soft dollar" commissions to pay for their bills. These commissions encourage advisors to trade your account and create more revenue for their firms. Finally, run from brokers and advisors who push their own in-house funds. They are given incentives to push these funds without regard to their fees or performance. This doesn't mean that all in-house funds are bad, only that these brokers and advisors are not always considering if they're the best investments for you.

Sloth can cause you to give any of these advisors a pass or fail to realize what they're up to. You may also lust after advisors with great reputations and who offer promises of incredible performance, overlooking their fees or questionable tactics. The best way to honor your financial advisor is by choosing one whose only fee is based on a fixed percentage of the assets you have under management and evaluate this individual based on comparisons with a reasonable benchmark.

Thou shall remain humble before the almighty market.

People are most vulnerable to the seven sins when they place themselves above the market. They are convinced they can outsmart it and fall for get-rich-quick schemes. They are certain that they know where the market is going and end up investing in the wrong direction.

No matter how well you do in the market in the short term, you always encounter portfolio-reducing surprises. For this reason, most of the best investors are confident but humble; they know the market can turn on them in an instant. They respect its power and attempt to manage it, but they also know it is unpredictable and volatile.

Humility is an antidote to all seven sins.

If you're humble, you will make an effort to combat your slothful tendencies, recognizing that the market chews up the indolent.

Being humble automatically moderates the effect of pride, allowing you to guard against thinking too highly of yourself.

Humility moderates gluttony, reminding you not to bite off more than you can chew.

It also helps you manage your envious tendencies, helping you be aware that every investor, no matter how successful in the moment, will experience the same losses as you have.

Humility demonstrates the futility of exacting vengeance or venting rage through an investment.

If you're humble, lust for a particular stock or financial guru isn't an issue, since you don't need to glom on to someone or something else to make yourself feel important.

And finally, being humble robs avarice of its power over you, decreasing the odds that you will want more than the market can provide.

Of course, this last commandment is probably the toughest to observe, since our society is constantly sending us messages that turn us into envious, angry, and proud investors. To observe it, remind yourself that you are investing in the market with the belief that it will deliver reasonable and significant long-term rewards, not unreasonable short-term ones. Approach investing with discipline and diversification rather than with seat-of-the-pants bravado. If you look at the market realistically and don't ask more from it than it can give, you will find it much easier to follow this commandment.

A Sensible Investment Strategy in a Volatile, Chaotic Era

Given the previous commandment, I would be the last person to predict the market's direction in the coming years. What seems reasonably safe to assume, however, is that we will see a market that reflects the fast-changing, world-shaking events of our era. I don't believe I'm going out on a limb when I suggest that the market is going to be full of surprises, that stocks everyone believed would do well will experience sudden downturns and stocks that no one had high expectations for will become big winners. Funds that have performed well for years will slide down a notch and turn in mediocre performances, and a little-known fund will become the hottest one on the Street.

In other words, the market will continue to be its unpredictable self, only more so. Given the increasing tension between nations, the continued terrorist threat, the interconnected global marketplace, the increasing demand for energy, the deficit spending of the U.S. government, and the looming environmental problems around the world, it doesn't take a genius to suggest that we live in uncertain, volatile times, and that the market reflects these times. On top of that, in excess of $1 trillion is in actively managed hedge funds, and this money will flow to any market where there is opportunity. Unlike mutual funds, this money can turn over with great speed. In addition, much of this money is leveraged—more funds are borrowed to increase the return of these bets. This "leverage in the system" will have a tremendous impact during any financial crisis.

A disciplined, long-term strategy makes great sense in this unpredictable environment. The Seven Sins method isn't the only conservative, diversified strategy out there, but it has the added benefit of protecting investors from their own, worst tendencies—tendencies that tend to come out in fast-changing, up-and-down markets. We may not experience an overheated market like the one that occurred between 1999 and 2000, but it's likely that we'll go through a similar "hot" period, and investors who are ruled by their greed, pride, or envy will likely suffer because a highly bullish market brings out these sins.

In fact, I expect that many opportunities will emerge in the coming years, and these opportunities must be approached prudently rather than rashly by investors with long-term objectives. There may be another wave of leveraged buyouts similar to what occurred in the late 1980s or a renewed merger-and-acquisition fervor. People will become rich, and this euphoria will drive normally rational investors to do things they would not normally do; their vulnerability to sin will be high.

There will also be crises and panics. No doubt, more "Enrons" will emerge or a hedge fund will blow up. On a large scale, we are bound to have events that have a dramatic, negative impact on the entire market. Think back over the last twenty years and you'll recall the 1987 crash, the 1990 bank crisis, the 1991 Gulf War, the 1998 Russian Government Bond default, the Long-Term Capital Management hedge fund failure, and 9/11. I have no idea what the next one will be, but I am certain that people will sell in droves when it hits; their various sins will gain power over them and cause them to sell reflexively and without objective analysis. The Seven Sins method helps impose objective analysis, manage reflexive selling, and take advantage of buying opportunities in down markets.

In calm, steady markets, investors are less vulnerable to the seven sins. They tend not to have as much to get angry about, to be proud of, to be greedy for, and so on. Rapid movement in the markets, however, stirs investors' emotions. We're likely to experience even more market swings in the future than we have had in the past. For this reason alone, people must resist the temptations that arise in periods of crisis or euphoria. Admittedly, resistance can be difficult, especially when market movements cause us to be even more slothful, vain, or wrathful than we normally are.

These are the times when investors make major mistakes and when you should be especially reliant on the seven sins framework. Use the stories in this book as cautionary tales and the advice as a hedge against emotional inflation. In the coming years, you're bound to find yourself in a situation where you're so angry at your broker who didn't warn you about a sector collapse or so eager to get in on all the action an up-market offers (such as gluttony) that you lose your cool, act too quickly, and make a significant error.

I cannot promise that the seven sins approach will prevent every error. It will, however, increase your odds of coming out ahead in the long run, and if you're like most investors who are concerned about retirement, your children's college educations, and other major life goals, long-term success is really the only true measure of your investing. Let other people win big and lose big in the short term. While they are still playing their zero-sum game, you'll be enjoying a secure financial future.

INDEX